Keep Going

---

30 Day Devotional

Bishop S.Y. Younger

The Shaunessy Group Inc.

Keep Going
Copyright © 2019 by The Shaunessy Group Inc.

The Shaunessy Group Inc
701 Thomas Road
Lynchburg, VA 24502

ISBN 978-1-7333128-0-6

PRINTED IN THE UNITED STATES OF AMERICA

Book Cover Photographer: Emmanuel Hammond (UK)

THIS BOOK IS DEDICATED

TO THE MEMORY OF

KYLON S. SMITH

My first Armour-Bearer and Diaconate Chairman

Table of Contents

Foreword

It has been said that "leadership is influence." To be an effective leader, one isn't required to possess the loftiest title, immeasurable opulence, or excessive acclaim. They must simply be granted the fleeting, precious gift of influence; the power or capacity to effect change in others. You can't buy influence or barter for it. You can't force it or obligate it. Influence instinctively shows up wherever there is great wisdom and character.

Bishop S.Y. Younger is an influencer. He is the Pastor of The Ramp Church International and the Vice Presider of One Way Churches International. He is a world-renowned preacher, musician, teacher, and songwriter. Bishop Younger is a dynamic prophetic voice who has been lauded for his charismatic and authentic style of communication. His influence is unique because it is so far-reaching. It expands across generational, socioeconomic, and cultural distinctions. He has the rare ability to relate and engage with a diverse audience. His ministry is littered with stories of bridges he has built across chasms where there once was significant variance. Bishop Younger develops leaders and oversees ministries around the globe; from Brazil, India, Guatemala, England, and all over the USA.

Bishop S.Y. Younger has taken his exceptional gift of communication to a brand-new arena by authoring his first book "Keep Going." This book is a powerful instruction manual on the art of navigating the difficult in-between stages of process. It teaches us that the fulfillment of our destiny requires intentional consistency and determined perseverance. "Keep Going" is a 30-day devotional that boldly proclaims the only thing that stands in our way of accomplishing all God has called us to do. Our decision is that no matter what we face, we must "Keep Going.

Bishop John Francis
Ruach City Church London, UK

Acknowledgements

I want to thank Jesus Christ, who is the same God of my childhood.

I would like to acknowledge my mother Dianne Younger who made so many sacrifices for me. The older I get, the more I realize. To my father, Frank Gilbert who has shown me what a man of God looks like. I love my entire Younger and Gilbert Family.

I would like to acknowledge Bishop Raymond Bennett who birthed me and my family into salvation. Thank you to Bishop Lorenzo Hall for raising me up in the ministry and covering me to this day.

I would like to acknowledge the children and grandchildren that God gave me. I'm working hard every day to be the person you already see me as.

I would like to acknowledge Pastor Marvin and Ashley St. Macary, Pastor William and Francine Westgate, the Board of Elders, Deacons and the entire Ramp Church Family. You have been my motivation to keep going.

I would like to acknowledge my One Way Churches International Family. We may not all meet in the same house, but we are all in the same church!

I would like to acknowledge Derick Monroe, my brother since the 10th grade. Thank you for talking me off of the ledge more than once.

I would like to acknowledge Enoch Paku, who pushed me to do this against my own desire. Special thanks to Mary Prather, Amber Martin and Denise Benton. To the entire Bishop Younger Ministry Staff, I'm thankful for how hard you work all year long.

I would like to acknowledge Cynthia Hall. Your tenacity fuels my faith.

I would like to acknowledge Minister Walter Virgil Jr. for posting that one-minute clip.

I would like to thank all of you who invested in my first book. Thank you for supporting my ministry all year long.
Blessings to you.

Introduction

When it comes to reaching our goals, our greatest challenge in life is often consistency. There are millions of reasons that come at us on a daily basis telling us why we should quit. These reasons always come to endorse our present fears and disappointments.

For most of us, consistency is the only thing between us and the fulfillment of our dreams. Even now as I am writing this book, there is a contractor next door to my office suite. This contractor is jackhammering a hole in the floor in attempts to install a bathroom. The only thing that has kept me at this desk amidst the noise is the fact if I don't stay at this desk, I'll never finish this book. In other words, I'm learning how to work through the noise and to be consistent in my efforts to move forward.

I have to keep. I know that sounds like an incomplete sentence, but the word "keep" means to continue or cause to continue in a specified condition, position, or course.

We have become professional starters. We fill every new season and new year with bold declarations that eventually turn into empty promises. These promises leave us sitting on the doorstep of our destinies, feeling disappointed in ourselves.

If you're not moving, you're stagnant—or even worse, you're stuck.

It is said that it takes thirty days to break a habit and thirty days to form one. So, let's take this journey together for the next thirty days to form better habits, to be consistent, to keep going.

Don't stop here on this page. Keep going.

Day One
Keep Praying

Prayer is often neglected, but consistent prayer is considered most essential and necessary for this journey. Prayer is simply communication with GOD. Although I just referred to it as simple, finding time to pray has become complicated. I have found that our lateral relationships are really a reflection of our vertical connection with the Most High. Many of our closest relationships suffer from a lack of or misinterpreted communication. We have become so busy that we are not productive in our communication. We find ourselves exerting a lot of energy but never hitting the target. When this starts to happen, we are in need of recalibration and realignment.

We take our cars to the mechanic to realign the tires when they start to turn and pull the car one way or the other. We might even take a clock or watch to a watchmaker for recalibration if the seconds seem to slip by too quickly. Similarly, we need to take time to recalibrate our spirit. For this kind of adjustment, we need to take our hearts to GOD in prayer.

If you have more tasks in a day than you have hours to complete them, you have to schedule prayer. I know how you might feel about that. For some, it will seem sacrilegious or disingenuous. For others, having to schedule a time to speak to GOD will lead to feelings of guilt.

But this has to be your start, because for some of you, if something isn't scheduled, it's not happening. I am a preacher, so I believe in praying without ceasing. This means having a heart for prayer and speaking to GOD all day. However, I'm not talking about the kind of prayer you pray while you are loading the dishwasher. This scheduled time of prayer is different. It is a scheduled time of uninterrupted prayer, a time with no distractions or thoughts that wander; even down to remembering to start the dishwasher before you leave for work in the morning.

The bible says that Adam met with God at a particular time each day. I know we could focus on where Adam failed, but let's look at where he stood instead. Adam named the animals and managed the entire Garden of Eden. Imagine what you can accomplish if you start meeting with GOD. Good things happen all of the time, but there are no great things that happen outside of prayer. KEEP PRAYING.

Praying consistently can be difficult when it doesn't seem like you are "feeling" the prayer. However, prayer is not an act of feeling. It's an act of obedience.

You can choose your own time to pray, but I like to pray in the morning before I start my day. When you start each day with prayer, it directs your day and settles your spirit. Many of us flood our minds with a to-do list as soon as we wake up. Some of us have family members who are ready to add to that list as soon as we open our eyes. So, in the morning, as you get to the restroom and before you check your Facebook messages, talk to GOD. You can't control what's going to happen on any particular day, but you do have power over how you will respond.

This type of power and discipline is the byproduct of prayer. I call it a byproduct because the main goal of prayer is to get closer to the Creator. The closer you get to light, the more you will reflect light. Getting closer to GOD also reveals purpose. I can encourage you to keep going, but if the purpose of your existence has not been revealed, <u>why</u> are you going? Who are you going for? The answers to these questions are revealed in prayer.

Before you start pouring out your list, remember not to make this relationship like the ones some of us are already in. Make sure you listen for Him. Give God space to speak. Get silent in His presence. You may come to realize that the purpose of prayer is not to change the will of God; as much as it is used to sustain you in His will. Even when it feels like it's not working, remember that prayer is not about feeling as much as it is about faith. Keep praying.

Day Two
Keep Speaking

God made us in His image and in His likeness. I believe this goes beyond having ears, a nose and a mouth. It speaks of our free will and our creative ability. When God brought forth the Heavens and the Earth, He did it by speaking. Pastor Joziel Koehler says, "Speaking is not just the way God communicates but it's the way He creates." If this is true and if we are made in His likeness, this means our words have power. Just as God created the world with His words, we create our world by the words that come forth out of our mouths. Proverbs 18:21 says, "life and death are in the power of the tongue." This means the words you choose to speak are directly connected to the life you choose to live. Studies have proven that positive and optimistic people live longer and healthier lives. Regardless of these facts, some individuals are committed to remaining negative. Have you ever tried to encourage someone who didn't want to be encouraged? No matter what you said in attempts to lift their spirits, they came up with another reason why they should still remain negative. These individuals never see the bright side of anything. Many people have been a victim so long, that even if their situation changed, their language would still reflect a defeated undertone. For example, you can live in poverty so long, that even after accomplishing financial stability, your language can still reflect a life of poverty. This is why a pessimistic person's happiness is always short lived. Their words have the tendency to take them back to the Lodebar of their comfort zone.

Learn how to rehearse words of life. If negative words attract negativity and death, imagine what positive declarations will gain. God is sovereign and all-powerful, but He doesn't impose His will upon us. We are partners with God when it pertains to our destiny. In John 5, Jesus walks up to the pool of Bethesda. There was a man there who had been paralyzed for 38 years. Jesus asked him if he wanted to be made whole. The answer to this question should've been an obvious given, but I found out that everyone who is sick doesn't desire to be better or made whole. Many people don't know what life is like outside of the assistance they receive. They are comfortable by being in constant despair. As soon as the paralyzed man was posed with this question, he started to rehearse his problem. He told Jesus about all the challenges he had and the reasons why he couldn't get healed. Does this sound familiar? Jesus instructed him to rise up and walk. When he responded in faith to Jesus, he was healed immediately. The next time you are posed with the potential of something better in life, instead of complaining start speaking. Let your words agree with Jesus.

There are many in the religious and secular world alike who talk about positive confessions, energy, and laws of attraction. I want to be clear in my stance. When I talk about energy, I'm referencing the realm of the spirit; our human spirit or the Holy Spirit. I also believe that the only true law of attraction is the Word of God. I will admit that these principles operate outside of our Christian circles or perspective because they are principles. However, it's the Holy Scriptures that communicate to us what we should be attracting. I'm not encouraging you to speak randomly or haphazardly but speak with purpose. Knowing the power of your words, speak with precise direction bringing forth the will of God for your life. Let your voice be the echo of God's voice. It's important that you also connect with people who are speaking the same thing. Corporate confessions yield corporate blessings.

Mark 11:22-24 "So Jesus answered and said to them, "Have faith in God. For assuredly, I say to you, whoever says to this mountain, 'Be removed and be cast into the sea,' and does not doubt in his heart, but believes that those things he says will be done, he will have whatever he says. Therefore I say to you, whatever things you ask when you pray, believe that you receive them, and you will have them."

One of my mentors, Pastor James Alfred Cage went home to be with the LORD some years ago. He pastored Eternal Hope Worship Church in Syracuse, NY. I still hold his testimonies and advice close to me to this day. He told me the story of when they were praying for a new church building. He found a location that they desired, but they didn't have the money. He began to pray and speak that the new facility belonged to him and the church. At the time the church was meeting on Beach Street. But every Sunday the congregation would stand up and say, "Eternal Hope Worship Church 1507 James

Street". This was actually the address of the desired new location. The people aligned their faith with their confession until things began to happen. Eventually Pastor Cage and his congregation moved into their new church. What are you speaking? Are your words brining destruction or life to your future? Pastor Cage is gone now, but there in Syracuse is a church that sits on James Street as a testimony of the spoken word. Say it until you see it. Keep Speaking.

Day Three
Keep Building

A builder is a person who constructs something by putting parts and materials together over a period of time. Builders are a special breed of people. It takes a special ability to discern the importance of different parts to make one cohesive structure. A builder is also one that can take a group of people from various walks of life and with a multiplicity of personalities and build a strong team. Building is the ability to take a vision and make that vision tangible. Building is taking what you perceive from the invisible spiritual realm and producing it in the visible material realm.

In one-way or another, we can be considered to be standing at an ongoing work site. You are either a builder, an opposer, or a watcher. At the worksite, builders are in constant motion. These are people who actually put their hands on the project or vision. Builders are not people who just offer advice on the sideline, but they are fully invested in the work. On the other hand, opposers are people who show up but, they do not show up to work. They are actually your critics. Jealousy is usually at the root of their expressions. Don't give a voice to the people who haven't made an investment. They will never be pleased or satisfied. Opposers will drain the energy of a builder, if allowed. Don't exhaust yourself trying to explain yourself to people who don't really desire to have an understanding. This brings us to discuss the watchers. They are not going to oppose you in your endeavor to build, but they are not going to help you either. These are people who may just admire you from afar. Your testimony and work ethic may actually be an encouragement to their faith. Remember that everyone who is not working with you is not necessarily against you. As a builder you will have enough enemies without needing to create any new ones.

When I think about men in the scripture who were builders, I think about Nehemiah. Nehemiah had a great job working for the king of Persia. Nehemiah's close proximity to royalty afforded him wonderful amenities in life. But one day he received news of the plight of his people. He was told that they were in Jerusalem, a city with torn down walls. This left them open and vulnerable to their

13

enemies who were capable of surrounding and attacking them. This information shifted Nehemiah to his core. At that moment he was burdened. A burden for purpose or cause is an overwhelming feeling that God puts on you that you cannot shake or escape. Many in our generation know what it is to pray for a blessing, but many fail to pray for a burden. A burden from the Lord is the yoke of the mandate placed on your shoulders that cannot easily be broken. There is no evidence that Nehemiah had any past experience in masonry, architectural design, or carpentry. But, when the news of the torn down walls tunneled through his ears, it activated the builder in him. He knew then that he had to do something. Exposure to a God-cause has the ability to unlock gifts and abilities in you that you didn't know you had.

When Nehemiah returned to the king's court, he did not return the same way. His whole disposition had changed. Looking perplexed in the presence of a king during ancient times, could have called for an immediate death sentence. Nehemiah still did not refrain. When the King noticed Nehemiah's disposition, he inquired of his reasoning. He expressed to the king the dire situation concerning his people and the desire to go and rebuild. Nehemiah found favor with the king. When you are consistent in your place of serving, you will find great favor when it's the appropriate time to build. The king gave Nehemiah the three things that every builder needed: time, protection and resources. I believe when we go before our King we should pray specifically. Every builder should pray for time to finish. Most of us feel like we have more on our plate that what we can handle. But, God will always give you time to accomplish what has been assigned. The LORD even answered Joshua's prayer and held the solar system still and he ended up winning the victory. Every builder should pray for protection. There's an old saying, "what you don't know won't hurt you." I totally disagree. I believe what you don't know can actually kill you. When I was growing up in the Pentecostal church, we would have testimony service. This was a time for people to publicly stand and give thanks to God for particular blessings. It was the norm for someone to stand and say, "I praise God for keeping me through seen and unseen danger." This was a statement acknowledging, with gratitude, that God protected them from things that they had no idea could have occurred. If you are a builder, you must be alert and aware of the spiritual warfare that is connected to your assignment. Ephesians 6:12says, "For we wrestle not against flesh and blood, but against principalities, against powers, against the rulers of the darkness of this world, against spiritual wickedness in high places." Nehemiah asked for royal documentation to support his journey back to Jerusalem. He knew the potential danger that came with this assignment. As a believer, the word of God is our royal documentation that declares, "No weapon that is formed against us shall prosper." When you are building a family, career, business, or ministry it affects everyone around you. Sometimes builders will be so focused on a project that they leave precious commodities exposed. Builders must also pray for the protection of their spouses, children, home and health. If the evil one can't get to you, he will try to attack what is closest to you.

Pray for resources necessary for what you are building. The resources you request should be greater in quality and quantity in comparison to what you have. The bible teaches us that we must be active in making our requests known unto God. Matthew 7:7 says, "Ask and it shall be given, seek and ye shall find, knock and the door will be opened unto you." There are some Christian teachers who discourage people from asking for material things. Praying for material things are sometimes deemed as carnal. Oftentimes, this perspective comes from people who have never really had a materialistic need. People with this perspective may often ask-Why do you need the car? Why do you need the large home? Why do you need the money? Your response should be, "It's because it is connected to the vision that God gave me." If it's God's will, it's God's bill. Vision comes from God, but provision comes from the Earth. As you build and pray, God will touch the hearts of people around you who will assist you and undergird the vision. Nehemiah requested the king's assistance to rebuild and his request was granted. If an earthy king released resources to his servant, how much more will our Heavenly father release to us- His sons and daughters?

Building is an act of obedience and not a source of instant gratification. The late Bishop Kenneth Moales Sr. once shared some insight with me. When they were raising money to build a cathedral, some people inquired about the money that was already spent. He instructed them to go look at the huge hole that was in the ground. The money was going towards building the foundation. Sometimes in the process of building, you may feel as though you're not getting anywhere. But remember the deeper the foundation, the taller the building. While Nehemiah was building, they mocked at the wall saying, "if a fox ran across it, it would tumble." But Nehemiah called his wall a good work. Remember it is not about what others say, but you must hold on to what YOU say. In the first year of our church, we had a storefront building with a leaky roof, broken up pews, white plastic lawn chairs, a rusty van, cubicles for offices, a funeral home registry for a podium, and only one bathroom- and it was AWESOME! We were building! There were many who mocked us because we were considered kids in their eyes. Little did they know; the kids grew up and the walls went up.

One of the most sobering truths I have ever had to come to grips with is that everyone does not want to see you succeed. Building exposes the hearts of people around you. There were those who came to Nehemiah bringing him news and rumors that brought his loyalty to the king in question. I could imagine that Nehemiah wanted to defend himself-and rightfully so. We all would want to defend ourselves when we've been wrongly accused. Instead Nehemiah asked, "Why should I stop working and come down to you?" In this passage, responding to critics can be viewed as coming down. How many times have you come down and wasted valuable time responding? The best way to defend your character is to maintain your character and keep building.

The spirit of discouragement will try to attack the mind of the builder. Every good builder uses a blueprint or some sort of architectural outline to keep the intended goal as a reminder. There are days in the life of the builder where you will have to remind yourself of why you started in the first place. It is God who called Nehemiah to this work of building. You have not been called by God until you have been inconvenienced by God. Nehemiah did not rebuild this wall for himself. After all, he lived in the comfort of the palace. Based off of this, you must understand that what you are building is bigger than you. The magnitude of your challenges may be a reflection of the weight of the impact and potential. What should have taken a long time to accomplish, maybe even years,

16

Nehemiah completed in 52 days. As you build, I pray that God grants you favor and divine acceleration in your building process. Keep Building.

Day Four
Keep Expecting

Have you ever gone through a situation that yielded a different result than expected? We have all experienced heartbreaks and disappointments as a result of letdown expectations. We have expected people to love us as we have loved them. We have expected promotions from employers that passed us up in favor of other candidates. Some people have even expected to be married by a certain age, only to find themselves still living a life of singlehood. The delay of expectations can cause one to barricade themselves in a cave of complacency.

Birthdays were not a big deal in our home growing up. Most of the time, I shared my cake with my cousins who were born around the same time as I. This may sound unbelievable, but my mother and I actually forgot my 11th birthday. It was almost a week later when we realized it. Let me be clear, this is not a sad story of neglect. My mother was a very hard-working mom, she just didn't make a big deal out of birthday celebrations. This was also the case when it came to her own birthday. One day I inquired of her lack of birthday enthusiasm. She informed me that as a child of eight children, her family simply did not have birthday parties. She remembered one specific birthday when she was expecting a watch. Her birthday came and went, and she never got one. This is a moment that she still remembers quite vividly as a woman in her sixties. I believe that particular memory produced a nonchalant, non-expectant disposition toward birthdays in general.

Expectation is defined as something to look forward to. To expect means to regard something as likely to happen. Expectations in their purest form is hope. Hebrews 11:1 says, "Now Faith is the substance of things hoped for or expected." We are designed to live with healthy expectations. A life without expectations is one that is trapped in a mundane routine or sequence of actions. I call this "treadmill living." Treadmill living is when you have adjusted to exerting energy, looking forward to going nowhere.

Sometimes, we stop expecting because we placed higher expectations on the wrong people. We all know what it feels like to be disappointed by people in whom you had expectations from. Being let down by humans will sometimes affect your expectations with God. There are moments when you will have to separate your expectations of God from your expectations of the people of God. We should never lose hope or a desired result with people we have a relationship with. Expectations placed solely in man can often become unhealthy, dysfunctional, and misplaced.

"My soul, waiteth thou only upon God; for my expectation is from Him."

Psalm 62:2

Although the arm of flesh may fail you, Romans 10:11 reminds us that whoever believes in Him will not be disappointed.

"It is better to trust in the Lord than to put confidence in man."
Psalm 118:8

Expecting can be a process that takes time. Process brings a level of discomfort and change. In our modern society, when a woman is pregnant with a child, we say that, "she is expecting." This expectation stretches her physical body. It shifts the very inner workings of her anatomy and physiology. Her expectation automatically places her in preparation mode as a nurturer. She must begin to change and monitor her health habits, her food consumption, and even her surrounding environment to protect and nurture the child she carries. When an individual is truly consumed in expectation, everything around them begins to reflect the desired end result. There is an Old Testament text that always speaks to me concerning expectations. In Isaiah 54:6, God speaks to Israel:

"Sing, barren woman, who has never had a baby. Fill the air with song, you who've never experienced childbirth! You're ending up with far more children than all those childbearing women." God says so! "Clear lots of ground for your tents! Make your tents large. Spread out! Think big! Use plenty of rope, drive the tent pegs deep. You're going to need lots of elbow room for your growing family. You're going to take over whole nations; you're going to resettle abandoned cities. Don't be afraid—you're not going to be embarrassed. Don't hold back—you're not going to come up short. You'll forget all about the humiliations of your youth, and the indignities of being a widow will fade from memory. For your Maker is your bridegroom, his name, God-of-the-Angel-Armies! Your Redeemer is The Holy of Israel, known as God of the whole earth.

The mere fact that God requires a song of praise from someone who is barren is indicative of His plan for them. If you notice in the passage, not only does He tell the woman to sing, but He also tells her to prepare. God's desire is revealed in His instructions. He says to her, "Make your tent large, spread out, and give it plenty of rope." It's often said that expectation is the breeding ground for miracles. Your preparation is a reflection of your expectation. Your ability to prepare speaks of a higher level of expectation and faith. One day at one of our churches, the parishioners and church workers were making plans and preparations for an event. They underestimated the number of attendees. When Sunday came, people were lined up outside trying to get into the building. The staff and team quickly realized they didn't have enough seating and found themselves rushing in efforts to accommodate the crowd at the last minute. This brings us to something to ponder upon. If the blessing of the Lord overflows to those who don't expect the overflow, imagine how much more would the Lord bless those with hope and great expectation?

What are you expecting? Does it line up with God's plan and desire for your life? Psalm 37:4 says, "Delight yourself in the LORD and He will give you the desires of your heart." If you really want to know the will of God for your life, the first key is to delight yourself in Him. Delighting yourself in Him will cause you to desire what He desires. Your desires will align with the desires of God. Your plans will align to the will and plan of God in prayer. Some of us lost a level of expectation because there were things we desired that were not aligned with the desire and the will of God. However, there are times when our expectations were not big enough. From this lower level of expecting, we risk lowering and reducing God down to our level of faith. Instead, I encourage you to bring your faith up to your God. In Acts 3, there was a man lame from birth. He was found

20

lying by a gate called Beautiful. Every day, he would ask for handouts, help, and assistance. He asked Peter and John for a handout and he expected to receive one from them. Peter responded to the man and told him that he did not have any money to give. He said, "But, what I do have, you can have also, In the name of Jesus Christ, rise up and walk!" The once lame man received strength in his feet and ankles. He began leaping and walked with them into the temple. He didn't get what he was expecting (money, assistance, and a handout), he received something far greater- healing and wholeness! Are your expectations too low? The man at the Beautiful gate was expecting something that would sustain him for a day. Be encouraged in knowing that Christ wants to give you something that will sustain you for a lifetime. Keep Expecting.

Read this prayer aloud:
Lord, heal the hurt of every damaging disappointment. Even the disappointments that prevent me from expecting. I believe the best is still yet to come. I consciously place my expectations on You, realizing, no good thing will You withhold from them that walk uprightly. Forgive me for placing my expectations on man instead of You. Today I have fresh expectations for my life and my relationship with you. Lord, I give you permission to exceed my expectations just like You did for the man at the gate. In Jesus name I pray, Amen.

Keep Moving

Have you ever been held up in traffic because of an accident? After looking at the gridlock from all of the traffic, you start praying because you begin to imagine the catastrophic nature of the accident. Eventually, you crawl bumper to bumper in your lane; inch by inch and approach the accident scene. There, you are surprised to see only a minor fender bender. Immediately, you are filled with conflicting emotions. On one hand, you are grateful that no one was hurt, but on the other hand, you are upset that you have wasted time unnecessarily.

You see, it wasn't the accident itself that backed up the traffic, it was the curiosity of the onlookers. To make ourselves feel better, we may say that it was the concern of the onlookers that slowed down the traffic. Most of us keep our doors locked with no inclination to get out and assist. We decide to take into consideration that the professionals are on site and are more equipped to handle the situation.

Many of us have been slowed down by things we have no control over or things that have nothing to do with us. We often stop just because we are curious- not because we care or have been called to stop there. We are slowed down by a roadside distraction that has added more time to our journey. So often, by the time we stop and waste time, we realize there's nothing to see, so we start moving again.

When my godson, Nicholas, was younger, he was a very good swimmer. His parents kept informing me of how well he performed at the swim meets. I decided I was going to support him at his next competition. When I arrived, he was surprised to see me and visibly excited. When he got in the water and began to race, I noticed he kept looking up out of the water to catch a glance of me and his competition. Unfortunately, he didn't win that particular match. Nicholas taught me something very valuable that day. You can't move forward while looking back. He was looking for my applause, just as any child would. But, when you're in a race, you can't be distracted; even by the noise of your cheerleaders. Slowing down for the affirmation of others can affect your momentum. Just like Nicholas, in life we have swimmers on the left and the right side of us. We must remember that we can't run their race. We must stay in our lane and keep moving.

You may have a genuine concern for the people around you, but you must remember that everyone is not your assignment. You're only allowed to work within your jurisdiction. If they are not your assignment, they will become your distraction. You are not the hero in everyone's story. As aforementioned we all have seen accidents on highways. Emergency personnel will inform you that too many people on the site during an accident can cause even more damage. Remove yourself. There are times when you have to trust the fact that there are other professionals in your vicinity who are more equipped to handle the situation. Apostle Paul says in 1 Corinthians 9:24-26, "Don't you realize that in a race everyone runs, but only one person gets the prize? So, run to win! All athletes are disciplined in their training. They do it to win a prize that will fade away, but we do it for an eternal prize. So I run with purpose in every step. I am not just shadow boxing."

You may be wondering what you should do. Well, if you want to make it to your destination before dark, keep moving.

Read this prayer aloud:
Dear Father,
Help me to discern what requires my attention.
Help me to remain focused and to look forward.
In this season of my life, I want to make up for lost time.
Lead me to the lane of consistent flow. Forgive me for all of the times I've tried to take your place as the hero in other people's lives. Give me wisdom to discern which situations have nothing to do with me and then stay out of them. Let me not be pulled into circumstances that hinder my mobility. LORD, I don't want to be stuck; please help me to keep moving. In Jesus Name. Amen.

Keep Learning

Life is a classroom. One of the best postures you can take is that of a student. It's often said that you should be a student until the day you die. Society tries to teach us that mastery is the height of accomplishment, but I believe a lifetime student is the superior position. The world around us is forever teaching us through people and experiences. Without being conscious and aware, you can easily walk over teaching moments that could forever change your life.

Study to be quiet. This is one of the scriptures over the years that I should've paid more attention to. I come from a family of talkers. We have strong fellowship with each other fused with aggressive speech; that's how I would describe it. If you were standing on the outside of our home and didn't know us, you would think we were having a brawl. In our family, if you have anything to add to an ongoing conversation you have to treat it like a train hopper, you must jump on board while it's still moving. I must admit this type of environment has probably caused us to misunderstand each other or gather misinformation over the years. The older I've become, I've tried to restrain myself and learn how to listen. Listening is where learning takes place. You can't effectively hear when you're talking. I've been given great opportunities to sit in rooms with older pastors, successful entrepreneurs, politicians and diplomats. In those moments, my silence has gained me the opportunity to learn more in an hour than years spent in a classroom.

It's a common saying that experience is the best teacher. I agree with this wise saying; however, I must also acknowledge that experience can sometimes be a painful teacher. Locked inside of every experience is a plethora of lessons. If applied, each experience can be carried as keys that will unlock future doors. Certain experiences are like prerequisite courses. You have to take them until you pass. Many of us would be further in life if we had learned the lessons of our past experiences. In grade school my English teacher would give our class a writing assignment. She would give us a date to turn in the rough draft and the date when the final draft was due. Once we turned in our rough draft, the teacher would return it to us with editing suggestions. My paper would be filled with red-ink proofreading marks. As frustrating as it was, if I learned from the remarks and made the necessary changes it was a sure thing that my final draft would be perfect. You may be experiencing a rough draft season in your life but learning from your mistakes can change the final outcome.

The challenge that some people have with learning new concepts or ideas is that they must be willing to unlearn what they already know. Many of our life lessons are like building blocks. This concept is seen in the core subject math. Basic math fundamentals such as subtraction and addition operate as a foundation for one's academic journey. If the foundation is faulty or in error, it must be re-laid. In the same manner, people are not open to learn new things if they feel it imposes upon the foundation of what they believe is true; even if it has been proven to be wrong. Instead of learning, there are those who find more comfort in familiarity. There is no honor in going the wrong direction just because you've went that way for so long. Instead, consider learning as a pursuit of doing things in a better way. A better way means becoming more efficient and effective. There are many reasons why individuals are not open to learning a better way. One reason is pride. Pride will make a person drive around a city lost in traffic for hours before asking for directions. Prideful people will attempt to sabotage a new plan or proposal; and if their destructive efforts are ineffective, they will attempt to assassinate the character of the presenter. The spirit of pride sits on the surface with insecurity lying below as its roots. The insecurity communicates that a new way of doing things or the arrival of a new person may compromise your image of sufficiency. People who are open to learning embrace new opportunities to increase in knowledge, and they see new people as an avenue for expansion.

I loved to learn but I was not the best student in school. If I was professionally tested, I most likely would have been diagnosed with Attention Deficit Hyperactivity Disorder, better known as ADHD. Symptoms of this include:

- Impulsiveness
- Disorganization
- Problems prioritizing
- Poor time management skills
- Problems focusing on a task
- Trouble multitasking
- Excessive activity or restlessness
- Poor planning
- Low frustration tolerance
- Frequent mood swings
- Problems following through and completing tasks
- Hot temper
- Trouble coping with stress

Some individuals will tell me not to claim a diagnosis such as ADHD, but when I look at this list of symptoms, at least ten of these symptoms have already claimed me. Whatever the case, I struggled in the classroom, but I didn't let it hinder me from learning. Find a way! Nothing is worse than watching everyone else get it and you're still left in the dark. I'm thankful for teachers, tutors, and coaches who worked hard to help me get through those challenges, but ultimately, I found out that learning was my responsibility.

There are several inspiring articles about men and women from the ages of 66 to 99 years old earning college degrees. Many of them had a passion for learning their entire life but decided to put education on the back burner to take care of their families. Even though they couldn't afford to go to college or attend university while raising their families, they kept their minds sharp by learning what they could. They would read newspaper articles daily, take trips to the local library, and find interesting books to read-they kept learning. Those who had children taught them the importance of education, pushed them to get degrees, and then realized it was important that they took their own advice. They didn't allow their age to dictate what they could or couldn't do. They kept learning and earned the degree of their choice. This should be a lesson to us all; never stop learning.

I'm always humbled by the stories of individuals who fought and even suffered for the opportunity to learn. My grandmother is one of the smartest people I know. However, her formal education never surpassed the third grade. As a child, she lived on a farm so far from the all-black one room schoolhouse, that she had to ride on the backs of the older boys who walked to school daily. When the boys became teenagers, they had to relinquish their education to work in the tobacco fields. This left my grandmother without any assistance to get to school. Knowing her story always made me feel guilty growing up when I took my accessibility to learning for granted. My local school was right across the street and there were days I didn't want to cross the road. I've preached in other countries around the world, and I've witnessed people travel for days by foot, bus, and even bicycles to hear the gospel and learn more about JESUS. We live in a country where there is a church on every corner, a Gideon bible in almost every hotel room, and preaching available at the click of a remote control and yet we fail to tap into the wealth of knowledge that lies at our fingertips.

Luke 10 tells the story of Jesus being in the home of two sisters, Mary and Martha. He was teaching his disciples and Mary who also sat at his feet. Martha was diligently working in the house and requested that Jesus tell Mary to get up and help her. Jesus' response was that Mary had chosen the good part and it wouldn't be taken from her. Many will choose to be busy, choose to be heard, choose to be popular and powerful but instead you must choose to learn. Many things in life can be taken from you, but what you truly learn will remain with you forever. Never allow yourself to get so busy doing and performing that you forget to learn along the way. Keep Learning.

Day Seven
No Mud No Miracle

When he had thus spoken, he spat on the ground, and made clay of the spittle, and he anointed the eyes of the blind man with the clay,
John 9:6

Jesus and his disciples noticed a man that had been blind from birth. The initial question the disciples wanted to know was, who sinned? The disciples did not ask if someone sinned, they wanted to know who. Bad fortune, sickness, or personal disaster has always been associated with either sin or some wrongdoing. They had to be surprised when Jesus answered and said no one. It shouldn't have been any surprise that the man hadn't sinned seeing that he was born blind. Jesus informed the disciples that this man had been born blind for the glory of God. This answer from Jesus can make one shutter at the complexity of the mind of God. The entire purpose for this man being born blind, growing up through the stages of adolescence- all the way to adulthood was so that God would be glorified. This man had never seen his parents or the world around him. Dr. Susie Wright says, "Maybe something that we have been rebuking is actually glory wrapped in affliction."

All throughout the gospels, the ministry of Jesus commonly included the performing of miracles and the healing of the sick. There were times when He healed individuals by laying hands; and then there were times when He just spoke the word. This occasion in the Book of John was different. Jesus spits in the dirt, making mud. He then takes the mud and applies it to the blind man's face. He then told him to walk to Pool of Siloam and wash his eyes. The bible said when he followed the instructions he came back seeing.

This is fascinating and yet very interesting. Jesus puts mud on the face of the blind man and then tells him to walk through the crowd. Consider for a moment what he looked like feeling his way through the crowd with a muddy face. For some of us our healing will take place privately. But there are other times when the LORD will use our lives to make a public display of His power. This publicity may cause you to look foolish to people as you blindly walk in obedience, while bearing the prescription of your healing on your face.

Here is a man blind from birth, who through Jesus' declaration isn't a product of sin. He has been forged with a deficiency so that The Glory of GOD may be revealed at an appointed time. Prior to this moment with Jesus, this blind man had suffered a life of no vision and poverty; learning to find contentment in begging while constantly feeling overwhelmed by the restrictions of his disorder. I could imagine him periodically wrestling with the thoughts of a better life. At some point he probably asked the Lord "Why did you make me like this?" So many of us can wholeheartedly connect with this blind man's state of mind.

One beauty of human life is when one of our senses are disabled, the rest are amplified. Though he never had the ability to see Jesus, he had amplified ears that heard all about Him and the many miracles He had performed. I can't begin to imagine the anticipation and the whirlwind of emotions that hit his stomach at the sound of the chatter of Jesus being near. The hysteria of desperation he must have experienced was probably untamed. While driven by such strong hopeful sentiments, I can also see him struggling with the probability of wondering if Jesus would even care enough about His life to change it.

As I read the scripture, it tells me that the blind man never presented himself to Jesus. He never had a friend or a group of friends to bring him to Jesus. Actually, Jesus saw him and begun discussing his life in detail with His disciples. Remember he had amplified ears, so if they were close enough to see that he was blind, they were close enough for the blind man to hear the content of their conversation. Jesus then answers a question that had plagued this man for his entire life. Finally, in an answer, the plan reveals what many could have a hard time believing GOD would orchestrate. Jesus plainly communicates, this blind man was born blind so that GOD could get The Glory out of his healing.

GOD trusts us with darkness because it creates a longing for His light. Thus, Jesus tells us, "As long as I am in the world, I am the light of the world" (John 9:5).

29

In the very next verse Jesus begins the resolution of this blind man's turmoil (John 9:6).

Jesus used mud.

Mud is a byproduct of water and dirt coming into contact with one another. The mud in this instance is a byproduct of Jesus' spit and the dirt from the ground the blind man is standing on. Ancient Hebrew traditions believed that there were healing properties within the spit of a Father's first-born son. It was believed that it stored medicinal purposes that had the ability to heal his Father's younger children. We can easily see how this can be transferred over into this story and more broadly to the healing of all those who are GOD's children. This account was not just for the blind man to be healed but it was for the revealing of who Jesus is. He is the begotten Son of God. When Jesus made the mud, he didn't mix his saliva with the dirt of some sacred place far from the Blind man. He used the dirt where he was standing. The Mud that will produce your miracle is manufactured the moment you allow His word to hit the dirt you're currently standing in.

No Mud No Miracle.

Several years ago, I was teaching a bible class in Syracuse, New York. I was teaching the students about the blind man in Mark 8. Jesus spat on this man's eyes and the man reported seeing men like trees. Then, Jesus laid hands on him and he saw clearly. We had a great class discussion that day. I would later learn that one of my students, Dr. Norton was historically regarded as the first black female optometrist in the state of New York. During one of our classes she informed me of something that really blew my mind. She told me that according to her study, the Blind Man's response to his sight being restored is theoretically accurate. The moment I heard that I employed her to expound to the class. She began to explain the medical sequence of events connected to sight restoration. Sensory signals are successfully processed within the cerebral cortex. The cerebral cortex is responsible for sight. Case studies consistently communicate, initial symptoms to be extremely blurry sight. A majority of case study subjects reported experiencing extreme light sensitivity and a significantly delayed ability to focus in on objects. This a result of cerebral cortex processing sensory signals dominated by an extreme intake of light. This state of elongated blurriness is a common stage of the cerebral cortex recalibrating itself. Once effectively recalibrated, the subjects now have the ability to focus in on objects and accurately assess their origin and function. When Jesus healed the blindman he was experiencing the recalibration within his brain. The goal is sight restoration. Embrace the mud and you will get the miracle.

Day Eight
Keep Your Heart Pure

Growing up, I often heard this saying, "Weep at the coming in and rejoice at the going out." This saying was referring to babies being born and people dying. However, it sounds like it should be the opposite. We usually rejoice when babies come into this world but weep when people leave us. The older I get, the more I understand. Without getting into the subject of original sin, we all agree that babies are in one or the other a blank canvas being drawn upon by the life around them. When a child is born in this world, they are fragile and innocent. This moment can be quickly saddened when you consider what they may have to face in life. As children, we are loving, trusting, optimistic, and hopeful until life happens. Life happens for some a little sooner than others. If you're wondering what I mean by "Life Happens," I'm referring to the moments of disappointment and hurt that we all encounter at some point. We experience these moments and the world around us through the eyes of our hearts. These disheartening encounters have the potential to take a world full of color and plaster it with a dark grayscale. Keeping your heart safe and pure can be easier said than done.

The gravity of emotionally inflicted pain is not what was done to you, but it has more to do with who did it to you.

King David endures this emotional distress, and it is clearly written about in Psalm 55:12-14 which states:

For it is not an enemy who reproaches me; then I could bear it. Nor is it one who hates me who has exalted himself against me; then I could hide from him. But it was you, my peers, my guide, and my acquaintance. We took pleasant counsel together and walked to the house of God in company.

There's no comparison to hurt like the one experienced from someone who was considered a friend or even a member of your family. Anyone in the world can say or do something to affect you, but it takes someone close to you to hurt you. The dynamics of your relationship with these individuals affect how you handle everyone outside of your nucleus. Ultimately your family becomes your first reference point for relationships. When you've experienced hurt from someone close, you will tend to see everyone else through the distorted lenses of a bruised and hardened heart.

Once people have been hurt in the same recurring experience or maybe from the same people; they began to build a callus around their heart. A hardened heart never allows people to genuinely get close to them. This emotional distance is called protection. Unfortunately, this often works as a disadvantage. Not only does this course of action keep hurt out, but it also keeps help from coming in. It may keep abuse from coming in, but it will also keep love at a distance-restricted and incapable of coming in. A pure heart is not a careless heart but a discerning one. A pure heart learns to discern, balance, and keep a healthy distance. You must remain close enough to people where they can hurt you but distant enough that it won't be fatal to who you are.

Matthew 5:8 says, "Blessed are the pure in heart: for they shall see God." In Matthew 18, Jesus tells the disciples that unless they become as children, they cannot enter into the Kingdom. When you lose the purity of your heart, it blinds you from seeing what God is doing. When your heart is hardened and contaminated, it hinders the flow of your creativity. A pure heart speaks of how you see people and the world around you. It's a God-view because God is pure.

Having a pure heart is not an indictment against you. There are times when you will feel foolish for being trusting. You may feel foolish for giving people an opportunity to hurt you because your heart and intentions are so pure. People will think that you are oblivious to the negative things that were said about you from the people that you are now assisting. You may be silent but that doesn't mean you're ignorant. It just may be that God kept your heart pure in the midst of it all. You will never be responsible for how people treat you. How they treated you is a reflection of their character and not yours. Joseph was sold into slavery by his own brothers. He was falsely accused by his master's wife and ended up in prison. Still yet, Joseph kept his heart pure. How do I know? It's evident because when he was in prison, he noticed the despondency of the other prisoners that were from the palace. He could've understandably been bitter, angry, frustrated, and skeptical of

33

everyone, but he remained pure enough to notice someone else's pain. This connection landed him in the palace.

How do you keep a pure heart in a society of takers where it always seems that someone is out to get you?

1. Remember you were the antagonist at some point. We have become so professional at being the victim that we sometimes fail to acknowledge that at some point in our lives, we have also been the villain. We have all inflicted hurt on someone else whether intentional or unintentional. Give people the grace you would want to receive.

2. Getting swallowed up in your offense will keep you stuck in the past. Keeping your heart pure will put you in place to feed those people tomorrow who hurt you yesterday. Ask Joseph. A person who has a pure heart doesn't want to see their enemies punished. Instead, they want to see them converted. Joseph eventually had to feed the same brothers who sold him. They were fearful that he would become vengeful, but he said to them, "You intended to harm me, but God intended it all for good. He brought me to this position so I could save the lives of many people."

3. Christ did it for us. We were his enemies but yet His heart toward us remained pure. Even when they were crucifying Him, He asked the Father to forgive them because they didn't know what they were doing. When we pray to be more like Him, we are asking Him to keep our hearts pure.

Day Nine
Keep Walking

The way you walk says a lot about you. There are people who are casual walkers who may stroll through a shopping mall to window-shop, and there are people who walk just to kill time. There are also people who I call treadmill walkers. Treadmill walking occurs when you exert a lot of energy in forward motion, but in actuality you never get anywhere. These are people who give you the impression that they are making major moves, but they always end up in the same place. Then, there are intentional walkers. Intentional walkers are people who have somewhere they need to be by a certain time. They are mission-minded and goal oriented. This type of walker is very focused with a specific destination in mind. Their body language communicates a sense of urgency. In order to maintain the schedule and accomplish the goal, this type of walker realizes that they must maintain a particular cadence. If there's any chance of having a conversation with an intentional walker, you must match their tempo. Slowing down for the wrong conversation can cause one to miss their purpose. You can be engaged with something that is harmless with good intentions and still be thrown off schedule.

"Let us strip off every weight that slows us down, especially the sin that so easily trips us up. And let us run with endurance the race God has set before us."

Hebrews 12:1

When Elijah gave his servant an assignment according to 2 Kings 4, he told him not to stop and greet anyone. Even if they were just greeting him, the servant's instructions were not to answer. The life of a child was at stake and he had to remain focused. What conversation has slowed you down? This is the season of your life to make up for lost time. Keep Walking.

I would like to say that I don't care what people say about me, but that would not be true. People who are the first to allude to the fact that they don't care, are those who struggle with it the most. We all want to be liked and accepted. It makes sense that we would have this desire being that God made us for relationship. We are

35

relational beings because God is relational. The opinions of others affect us and to some extent they should. However, we must keep it in perspective. The bible instructs us to be sober. When the word intoxication is mentioned, we quickly make a mental reference to alcohol or some other substance being abused. However, many people are easily inebriated or even addicted to the acceptance of other people. They will go to the extreme of attempting to reinvent themselves to win the applause of others. This puts a person in a dangerous place. Lecrae Moore said, "If you live for people's acceptance, you will die from their rejection."

Opinions can be very cheap because everyone has one. When you are a person of drive and vision, there will always be individuals who will have an opinion about the way you should do things. I refer to their sentiments as merely opinions, instead of advice, because real advice should come from trusted advisors. Often times, those who have a lot of unrequested opinions are those who have little to no experience in your related field. Before you allow the opinions of others to sway or pull you, check the source. If they are not a trusted and proven voice in your life, do not give their opinions great weight. Learn the art of caring about what people say without always carrying it. Remember that this comes with the territory.

I started our church in 2005 in a very small town. We were a group of young people who were passionate, zealous, and very controversial. Controversy was not the label we sought, but it became a byproduct of our movement. Everything about us seemed to be controversial, especially within our community. For example, the average age of our church members was twenty years old. I was a single pastor which was also considered taboo. Marriage was seen as a way of solidifying your manhood and maturity. On top of it all, in a very conservative religious community; our very expressive, emotional, and Pentecostal style of worship caused quite a stir in many neighborhood discussions. I had a very devoted church member, who out of her loyalty, would always keep me updated with recent community comments about me and the church. Eventually I asked her to refrain. It started to affect my momentum and slow down my rhythm. I had to learn how to keep walking.

Anyone who has experienced any level of success has simultaneously experienced some level of controversy. If you can't handle controversy, you will never experience real success.

The earthly ministry of Jesus spanned three years. During that period of time, Jesus himself was successful, but very controversial. In the midst of it, He stayed focused on the assignment. He came into the Earth with the purpose of redeeming mankind. He healed the sick, he fed the hungry, but He kept walking. They called him the devil and a blasphemer, but He kept walking. The multitude would throng him with their praise and adoration, but he kept walking. He was betrayed and denied, but yet He kept walking. The crowd shouted, "Crucify him!" He took up His cross and He kept walking; all the way to his destination, Golgotha. May we be so focused on our assignment that when the sound of the crowd changes, we never lose our rhythm. May we seek to please The One who sent us. At the end of our performance, we can drop the mic and walk off, knowing that the applause comes ultimately from The One who matters.

"Looking away from all that will distract us and focusing our eyes on Jesus, who is the Author and Perfecter of faith [the first incentive for our belief and the One who brings our faith to maturity], who for the joy [of accomplishing the goal] set before Him endured the cross, disregarding the shame, and sat down at the right hand of the throne of God [revealing His deity, His authority, and the completion of His work]."

Hebrews 12:2 AMP

Day Ten
Keep Forgiving

Often times, we hold on to unforgiveness as a reward to ourselves and as a punishment to others when in reality, the punishment is really ours. We often revert back to our adolescent years in which we bring attention to our wounds caused by others in an attempt to justify our anger. Let me be clear: I'm not asking you to be desensitized toward your pain or the pain of others. I'm just encouraging you to ask yourself how long should you bear a grudge. Unforgiveness turns into bitterness, and bitterness is like drinking poison yourself but waiting for the other person to die. Would another sentence discussing how unforgiveness is self-detrimental be helpful here?

Your unforgiveness doesn't just affect you or the person you're not forgiving; it infects your whole circle of influence. Often times, we don't realize that we are making our present pay for what our past did to us. When we walk in unforgiveness, we never experience total healing. Therefore, someone who is not healed is someone who is bleeding. Many of us have left a trail of blood in our relationships because we are not healed from past hurts. Forgiveness, though, removes the bullet so that healing can start taking place. Many of us want to heal, but we don't want to go through the pain of extraction. You are not healed when you can't talk about it. You are not healed when you have to dodge people. You are not healed when you talk about it in a venomous manner. Forgiving someone doesn't mean it didn't happen. Rather, forgiveness is my response to the wrong done to me. There are many things that will happen in life that you have no control over. The only thing you will be able to control is your response to those things.

I choose to forgive. What's my alternative? It's either forgive or keep myself locked in a prison of my own emotions. A prison where I'm playing the part of the inmate and warden simultaneously- never realizing that I have the power to set myself free when I'm ready.

I was molested around the age of seven by an older family member. I didn't speak of it for almost a decade. I went through what everyone else who endures such an encounter goes through. I dealt with guilt because I remember at that age it was like an exciting adventure. I dealt with shame because I felt it was wrong, not understanding that it wasn't my shame to carry. As I grew up, I went for years without seeing this family member because he lived in another state. I became a preacher, and by being the first one in my family I was proudly the preacher of the family. I received a phone call that a different member of my family had died. I realized that this was going to be the first time I would interact with the person who molested me since I had become an adult. I didn't know how I was going to react. When I walked into the funeral home, my heart was beating so fast that I thought I would pass out. But, then a sudden/gradual peace came over me. He stood and embraced me and spoke kind words to me, and I was able to embrace him back. Unfortunately, some time later, he was murdered, and I was called upon to preach, but this time, I was to preach at his funeral. By the grace of God, I was able to preach the good news of Jesus that day and many came to know the LORD. I was shocked. I was waiting for some sort of wave of emotion from my childhood to overcome me. When suddenly, I came to the revelation that I had already let it go. The blessing is that I didn't wait for him to die before I moved on. I can talk about this childhood experience now because it's a scar, not a wound.

There's a dent in the middle of my forehead from my childhood where I was told that I hit my head on the corner of a coffee table at the age of two. As an itinerant speaker my image is plastered on marketing placards on a regular basis. It's always funny to me how some media specialists take it upon themselves to airbrush away my dent. In their minds, I guess I look better without it, but I say to media and marketing, "Put my scar back! It's now a part of me. It's a scar. You can touch it, and it doesn't hurt anymore. My scar is my testimony." Jesus rose on the Third Day with all power in His hand. He walked through walls with a glorified body and still chose to leave the scar as a testimony to Thomas.

Will you display your scars, too?

There is someone who needs to hear the testimony behind your scar. You won't be effective holding on to unforgiveness. It will stifle your creativity and cause you to miss out on life, love, and happiness. Life will come with many offenses, disputes, hurts, attacks, misunderstandings, and neglect-either knowingly or even unknowingly, but you must posture yourself in forgiveness. Posturing yourself in forgiveness means that you must be willing to forgive someone who didn't even ask. Accept the apology that you may never even receive. To keep forgiving means to practice forgiving consistently with your mouth (often several times) until your heart aligns with it. Forgiving someone doesn't mean that person will maintain the same position in your life, but it does it mean you have taken the power of how it's being positioned in your heart. Choosing to forgive means you will keep going towards the goal of operating from a healed place, a whole place, a hopeful place.

Day Eleven
Keep Giving

On September 13, 2004, I was sitting in my apartment watching television. The Oprah Winfrey Show came on and she gave members of the studio audience a brand-new car. I got up off the couch and went immediately to my prayer table up against the wall. This makeshift altar was nothing but a little wooden coffee table that had crosses, a bible, and a bottle of anointing oil sitting on top. I know this specific date because I recorded an entry in my prayer journal that day. It read:

"Lord, today Oprah gave away eleven cars to people who really needed them. LORD I WANT TO DO THAT! I want to bless your people. I just wanted to jot this down for remembrance.
                                                        September 13, 2004

I've always seen myself as a generous person. I don't say that in a boastful way, for in most part I owe it to my upbringing. We never had a lot growing up, but whatever we had everyone was always welcomed to it. Giving has always been something that invigorates me. I've always enjoyed seeing the appreciation or the relief on someone's face when they've received something they really needed. I know there are blessings connected to the act of giving. But seeing someone's day or life changed is a blessing within itself. If being a Christian is all about being like Christ, this means our whole entire life should be about giving. We should forever be looking for ways to give of ourselves, our talent, and resources.

A lot of times people feel like they can't be a giver because they don't possess what someone else has. We can all be givers on whatever level we're on. In 2004, when I was watching the Oprah Winfrey Show I was a college student with a minimal income, sharing an apartment with a roommate. All I knew, once I saw that show, was that I wanted to be wealthy so I could do more for other people. Shortly after I was blessed to be able to acquire another vehicle. I had driven around my Honda Accord for several years and it was still driving well but this new vehicle was a Lexus GS300. It's the car I'd always wanted, and it was a blessing how I acquired it. I still had the Honda and I was considering selling it, but I hadn't made a concrete decision. Until one day, I received a knock on the door, and it was a nearby neighbor. I had passed him on the road nearly every day, greeting him with a head nod but we didn't know each other personally. Now he's at my doorstep and we are officially meeting and exchanging names. He made a reference that he noticed I had gotten a new vehicle and was wondering if I was going to sell my older car. He informed me that his car had broken down and that he was having an issue getting to work and transporting his family. I told him I would consider a price for the car and for him to come back the next day. As soon as he left, I started to do research to find out the car's appraisal value. Then, I heard a very non-abrasive inner voice say to me, "Give it to him." I quickly tried to dismiss this tugging voice. I started considering the additional needs I had and how the money from selling the car could assist. No matter how much I tried to shut out the voice, I couldn't shake the feeling. I even toyed with the idea for a second that maybe the devil was telling me to do this. I now laugh at those sentiments. Why would the devil tell me to bless someone? It finally came to me. I remembered the day I told GOD I wanted to do what Oprah did. However, I was thinking more along the lines of giving a car away once I had at least ten in my arsenal.

I finally surrendered to the fact that with only two cars, God wanted me to give one of them away. Now I had a new struggle. Who should I give it to? I knew the neighbor was the first one to make a request, but I didn't really know him. There were people in my family and church that I knew personally that could benefit from receiving a car. I thought it made sense to give it to one of them, but I'm consistently reminded that His ways are not our ways. I knew it was God's will for me to give the car to the neighbor. I believe in giving to family and friends but giving to people that we are familiar with sometimes obligates them to a certain level of loyalty to us. Spontaneous and discretionary giving to people who we have no close relationship with ensures that God gets all of the glory. The next day when he showed up on my doorstep, I handed him the keys. He was so confused. It took him a few minutes to digest that someone he didn't know was giving him a car. His facial expression that day was priceless. There was no Facebook live and no large audience present to clap, but I knew God was pleased. In that moment I knew I had done the will of God because an overwhelming peace came over me like a warm blanket.

A few months later my car broke down. It was with the mechanic for months. When I finally got it back someone hit it in the parking lot of the university, and it was declared totaled. After I obeyed God and gave away one of my cars, I was then left with no vehicle. The only semi-reliable transportation I had was an old church van that was donated to our small church plant. I believe there's a blessing that takes place when you tithe and sow seeds but it's not always instant. Once a farmer plants a seed, he doesn't stand over top of it, he moves on. He trusts the process. The first stage of the seed takes place underground. Just because you don't see a harvest doesn't mean your sowing didn't work.

So, let's not get tired of doing what is good. At just the right time we will reap a harvest of blessing if we don't give up.

Galatians 6:9

The LORD has blessed me over and over down through the years since 2004. Several years ago, after traveling and speaking, I returned home to a request from a married couple in my church to meet with them. When I made myself available to meet with them, they handed me the keys to a car and told me I had no payments. I tried to refuse such a gift but then the LORD brought back to my remembrance the car I had given away.

The way you give and the attitude in which you give is a reflection of your trust in GOD. This experience taught me that our proclamations and vows will be tested. If you won't give on this level, you will never be trusted to give on another one. Even when it doesn't make sense to you, follow the voice of GOD. When you give it always comes back. It may not come back in the form or manner you gave it, but it will return. Genesis 8:22 says, "While the earth remaineth, seedtime and harvest, and cold and heat, and summer and winter, and day and night shall not cease." It may come back quickly, or it may take a while, but keep giving. Obedience is your responsibility and the results belong to GOD.

43

Day Twelve
Keep Helping

We live in a very Hedonistic culture that's layered in our language of modern expressions that we should look out for ourselves. I understand the importance and responsibility of self-preservation; however, I don't believe we are truly successful until we have made someone else's life better.

I believe in helping others. Helping others has been both my greatest strength and greatest weakness in life. Over the years, I've tried to learn "when" to help and "who" to help. There have been many who requested my oversight or mentorship in one way or the other. I've always had the challenge of trying to discern who is worthy. I'm not referring to who is worthy of me, but who is worthy of one of the most valuable commodities that I possess in this earth: my time. Once I lose time, I can never get it back. I need "me" time, but I also need—and want—to be a good steward over the time that has been designated for me to sow into others.

When people approach me with their requests for my counseling or coaching, they often all say the right things, which makes it very complicated to decipher between the worthy and the unworthy, the ready and unready. In times past, it was challenging for me because I would be moved by their request combined with a strong rhetoric of humility laced with flattery. But very quickly, I would learn that people can say the right things with the wrong motives.

Acts 16 tells us a story of how a young woman was walking behind Paul and some of the brethren telling everyone how they were mighty men of God. The Bible said that after many days Paul got annoyed or grieved by this until he finally turns around and casts the evil spirit out of the woman. That story escalated quickly didn't it? Why would Paul rebuke this woman? How did he even know she had a demonic spirit? She was saying the right things but with the wrong motives. The scriptures say that her master was making money off of her demonic psychic ability. Her attempted association with the apostles was no doubt an agenda to increase their influence and money. There are times where hurt will come under the disguise of help.

Similarly, when asking for help, some people would remind me of who I was when I was just a young man seeking for answers or oversight. Such reminders would cause me to be emotionally drawn in and be more willing to help. We are drawn to people with pleas, and I categorize this as having a pastoral heart. This is a heart that's always willing to help and rescue whomever they can. This pastoral or shepherd's heart is what will cause one to dive in to recover someone without a second thought. It's in our instincts.

Then there's another aspect of us. It's the part of us that is always playing out scenarios, looking ahead, weighing people's motives, discerning their hearts, and engaging carefully. I call this perspective prophetic vision.

I don't think this represents two different people but two different aspects of the same person. Some people are weighed more on one side than the other. We are all very willing and very hesitant at times depending on the situation. There are times where this complexity in us creates significant conflict. This is when our heart is being pulled in the direction of someone's need or desperation, while your prophetic vision warns you that responding is not a good idea. There are times when our pastoral heart blurs our prophetic vision. You hope to always get it right, but the truth is that you won't. There are times you're going to help people and it will feel like a waste of time. In those times, remember that you will never be responsible for how they responded to your efforts. Your character is reflected in how you tried to help.

So how do you know when someone genuinely wants your help? You will know that someone is your assignment or wants your help in the way that the person responds to your directives. If he or she hasn't followed your last set of instructions, then that person is not ready to be helped. I often say to people, "I can't beg you and bless you." This doesn't mean that the person will not relapse or make bad decisions in the process. People need help for a reason. The need for help means they have come to the end of their ability to get through something on their own. However, keep in mind that your position is to equip the other person, not to expend all of your own resources. If you find yourself more invested emotionally, spiritually, and financially in their progress than they are, you are no longer helping. At this point, you're either controlling them or being used.

The posture of the lifeguard at the beach speaks to me. The lifeguard realizes that everyone who is screaming at the beach is not drowning. Some people are enjoying what they are in. A good lifeguard has to be able to decipher between the sounds. In a case where there is a real emergency, the best life guard is a dry one, the one who is constantly surveying everything and only gets in the water to save someone when it's absolutely necessary. This is important because there are times when the people who are drowning will, in their frantic and desperate attempt for survival, fight the very people who are trying to help them.

Although there are many risks that accompany helping, there are also benefits. You get a front row seat to an individual's recovery and success. There's something very rewarding about participating in such transformations. There is a sense of fulfillment that we experience when we help others. Helping others doesn't make you weak. Actually, it takes a strong person to carry another's burden. There is no one who has accomplished anything in life without someone helping them. Let this understanding be your motivation. Someone took the time to help you even when it was inconvenient for them. Maybe there are some people you need to text or call and say thank you. The greatest way you can show your gratitude is to help someone else. Keep Helping.

Read this prayer aloud:

Lord, today I ask you to give me your heart for people. Help me not to be desensitized when I'm no longer moved with compassion. Give me a discerning heart. Allow me to know who my assignment is and who my distraction is. Grant me the wisdom needed to help someone else. Deliver me from the need to be a hero in the face of flattery. You are the Savior, so just allow these hands to be the conduit of your love and power. Thank you for the people you have sent in my life over the years to help me get where I am today. Now

I ask you to make the hearts of those to whom I am sent receptive. May all things be done to Your glory and honor.

Day Thirteen
Keep Believing

Believing is defined as an action, state, or occurrence. Our beliefs are comprised of our ability to trust, have faith, or confidence in something or someone. Beliefs are firmly held convictions and acceptance that something is true or that something exists. It's inclusive of one's standpoint, stance, perspective, and way of thinking.

Now the Spirit speaketh expressly, that in the latter times some shall depart from the faith, giving heed to seducing spirits, and doctrines of devils;

1 Timothy 4:1

The scripture tells us that a sign of the latter days would be people departing from the faith. It didn't say they would necessarily depart from the church, but they would depart from the faith. This means there would be a generation of people who I call unbelieving believers. These are people who will participate in religious activities but don't actually believe in the scriptures or the power of God. 2 Timothy 3:5 says "Having a form of godliness, but denying the power thereof: from such turn away." This is why is it important to pay close attention to the types of teachings. You must examine your upbringings to ensure that they align with the Word of God. Just because it's what you were always taught, doesn't make it right. As a believer, God's word should be the foundation of your belief system and not what's trendy. Anything that is contrary to God's word will contrarily shape your beliefs. This requires us to be deliberate, aware, discerning, and intentional when it comes to entertaining other teachings, doctrines, and people's convictions when shaping our own.

What you believe must be established outside of you and not just your own inward council. Anything worth believing can handle the test of confrontation. In addition, we shouldn't allow disappointments and defeats, past experiences, or setbacks to alter our belief systems or stop us from believing all together. There are many who began to question the very existence of God once they experienced their own moral failures, hardships and limitations. Just because there are flaws in us, it doesn't mean there are failures in GOD.

Your beliefs are not your feelings. Do not build your belief system based off of your feelings or emotions. It's been said that most believers get their theology from the songs they sing more than the scriptures they read. Music plays an awesome part in the body of Christ, but make sure the truth of God that you know goes beyond the chorus line of your favorite worship band. Your beliefs and ability to believe have to do with the mind. Your feelings and emotions have to do with your heart. The bible says that the heart is deceitful above all things and beyond cure. Who can understand it? (Jeremiah 17:9). Let your beliefs affect your feelings and not the other way around.

I would have fainted unless I had believed to see the goodness of the Lord in the land of the living.
Psalm 27:13-14 KJV

Our belief system goes beyond what we believe about God, but it's all inclusive of what we believe he's capable to do in our lives. Maybe we are now fainting in despair because we've stopped believing. There's a saying that says people don't believe anything they hear and half of what they see. Even some "believers" have become very cynical. Stop focusing on your limitations and focus on God's power. A father came to Jesus, pleading for his son who was demon-possessed. In Mark 9:23 "Jesus said unto him, If thou canst believe, all things are possible to him that believeth." He asked Jesus to do something for his son but then Jesus put it back on him. The man's honest reply captured my attention and heart. He said "Lord I believe but help thou my unbelief." Seems like the father had an inner conflict. On one hand he believed because it was Jesus, but on the other hand within his conscience, he seemed to revert back to the number of many years his son had been tormented with no change. It seems like the faith he supplied was enough for Jesus to respond and to bring deliverance to his son. You don't have to wait for all of your doubts to leave before you believe. No matter how many setbacks you've had, still believe. God can change everything with one word.

But without faith it is impossible to please him: for he that cometh to God must believe that he is, and that he is a rewarder of them that diligently seek him.

Hebrews 11:6 King James Version (KJV)

There is a classic song written in the 1970s by the famous American rock band- Journey. This group acclaimed their success from a hit song called, Don't Stop Believing. This hit song remains a top selling track today and continues to be heard in our present culture and society. The history and details behind the original song are quite inspiring from the songwriter's perspective. The writer, Jonathan Cain recalls that as an aspiring musician, he left his hometown of Chicago for Los Angeles, in hopes of becoming a successful musician. When those dreams and plans seemed impossible, he phoned his father for help. He asked his father, "Should I just give up on this thing and come back home?" His father replied, "No, no, don't come back home, Stick to your Guns. Don't stop believing." The songwriter doodled the phrase "Don't Stop Believing" in his notebook where he stored all of his songs. He would frequent this notebook for inspiration to pen his music. He kept being drawn to this phrase- "Don't Stop Believing" when he grew discouraged after working to write his music. He would visit this phrase in the back of his notebook so frequently that he ended up jokingly creating a tune. This tune would end up being the chorus to the song and the rest is history. The song went on to climb the charts and it continues to be sampled by many artists in the music and entertainment industry today. A lesson can be learned from Jonathan Cain's history behind the making of the song. Keep frequenting, keep rehearsing your reminder to Keep Believing. Write this phrase on the mirror in the bathroom or write it on the dashboard of your car on a post it notes. Record it somewhere as a visual reminder for yourself. I believe it will inspire you to pen/create some of your own greatest creations, achievements, ideas, and innovations. The phrase "Keep Believing" is more than a phrase, but it is a reminder. I want to challenge you to rehearse this reminder. Consider this as your cue to intentionally keep believing.

Day Fourteen
Keep Changing

It's the one thing that's inevitable. It's the thing that's often hardest to do. It's the thing some people fear more than death itself: Change.

We don't like change because we are creatures of habit. We like to be able to control our environment, and we fear what we ultimately can't control. Change itself can be a very painful process, but it's an experience in life that's necessary. When cleaning the house and doing chores, my mother would remind us that a place is not really clean until you change things around. Keeping things in the same place without change every so often allows things to hide under the dust that can settle over a stagnant space. A lack of change can cause a loss of influence and the refusal to change can lead to extinction.

Not only should you be open to change, but you should also pursue it. We should always be in pursuit of a better way to live our lives. You should want to change into a better version of yourself. Notice, though, that I didn't say a *different* you but a *better* you. When the caterpillar changes into a butterfly, he doesn't become a different creature. He simply changes into the form of himself that he was designed to become. Sometimes pride and fear causes people to hold on to their old methods and behavioral patterns under the guise of what we call "being authentic" or "being ourselves". Crawling may have been your initial existence, but you were always designed to fly from the beginning. Apostle Paul says in 2 Corinthians 5:17 that when we come into Christ that we become a new creation in Him. The writer also says that those He called, He already knew, and He predestined them. But don't let these words allow your mind to drift. Listen to this. This tells you that as you come into Christ, you not only receive a revelation of who He is, but you also get a revelation of who you are. When you commit to being open to change, you will be introduced to the form of you that you were already designed to be before the beginning of the Earth.

My grandparents lived in the same house. It was a small house nestled by the railroad tracks in a small, one-stoplight town in Virginia called Gretna. The house had undergone many renovations and modifications over the years, but it was on the same parcel of land. One day after landing at Washington Dulles Airport after a trip to Mongolia, I saw that I had a voicemail from my Aunt Margie. She said that my grandmother wanted to meet with me, which was an abnormal request. I drove straight to my grandparents' home, and after a few moments of small talk, my grandmother hit me with her plan. Without any decorative speech my 80-year old grandmother informed that she had decided that she and my grandfather were moving. But they weren't *just* moving. They were moving to Lynchburg, Virginia to be closer to me. Originally, I thought she was joking, but I soon realized that she wasn't. She said to me with confidence that God had spoken this plan to her. I had always promised my grandparents that I would take care of them when they got older, but I guess I never realized that time had come. As the oldest grandson, I did my due diligence to find a home that was large enough, and I did, but that was only half of the battle. I come from a very large, loving and heavily opinionated, southern African American family. This is my way of saying everyone was not on board with this decision. My grandmother was getting older, and my grandfather was in the early stages of dementia. Although many thought it was ludicrous for my grandparents to move to a new home in a new city at their age, it didn't stop my grandmother from packing. At 80 years old, she wasn't afraid of change.

What excuses are you giving that you can't change? What voices are around you that are keeping you from change?
By the way, when I moved my grandmother to my city, I had to retrieve her vital records from the state. This included her birth certificate. I don't have time to go into all the details in this book, but to my amazement, I discovered that she actually was born in Lynchburg-80 years prior. Sometimes when we are making changes, we feel as though we are getting further and further away from our destiny, but the next step of drastic change could actually be bringing things full circle in your life. Keep changing.

Day Fifteen
Keep Worshipping

Worship is a word that we use often in our Christian vernacular. It's often used to describe our preference of music style or even our emotional expressions within a church setting. The truth is every human being is an innate worshipper. It's the way God made us. Every human may not be religious, but they are worshippers. Even atheists are worshippers. Those who deny the existence of God because they can't prove or dissect Him actually are worshippers of their own intellect. Anything that we exalt above the true God becomes our god. When God was ready to establish a system of worship, he pulled a man by the name of Abraham off to himself. He instructed him to leave his country, kindred, and he would make him a father of a great nation. Abraham and his wife Sarah were barren and had no children, but God promised them a son. Being in their old age, Abraham and Sarah laughed at the notion that they would have a child. When she had the child, they named him Isaac which means laughter. What a beautiful way to end the story, but this is not the end. God later required of Abraham to bring this very son to the top of the mountain to lay him down as a sacrifice. Yes, you read it correctly. God gave him a son and then required the same son as a sacrifice. Abraham prepared to go on top of Mount. Moriah. He looked at his servants and instructed them to stay at the foot of the mountain because he and Isaac were going up to worship.

There are a few things that spoke to me in this. When it came time to bring a sacrifice, God required them to come to Mount Moriah. This indicates that there is a designated place of worship. Not only was it a designated place, but it was a place they had to ascend to. I'm not suggesting that your worship is limited to a geographical place with a steeple and stain glass windows. However, I do believe worship is required at a certain place in our hearts. The address of the sacred place of worship is the posture of our hearts. Just as they climbed the mountain, I believe true worship takes place at a heightened place in our minds and thought patterns. Psalm 24:3 asks the question, "who shall ascend unto the Hill of the LORD......" I love the concept of the modern casual church where its intentions are to make everyone feel welcome to come. On the other hand, I'm sometimes concerned that casual church has produced a casual approach to God and the things of God. We can become so people accommodating that we can become God-offensive. It's not about giving God what we want but it's about giving Him what He requires. We must ascend to worship. A heightened place of ascension is a greater sense of consciousness and sensitivity to the realm of the spirit. We also read in this biblical narrative that Abraham leaves his servants at the foot of the mountain. This shows that everyone can't go with us to our place of worship. Worship is intimate.

One of the most profound revelations I received from this passage of scripture is that Abraham knows what God is requiring. He's requiring his son as a sacrifice and Abraham calls it worship. This is not just a powerful statement but a great understanding. It's not true worship until it costs the worshipper something. David says in 2 Samuel 24:24: "I will not offer burnt-offerings unto Jehovah my God which cost me nothing." Job after finding out that all of his children died in one day-worshipped God. Worship is more than a song or a physical gesture. Actually, those things can only serve as an expression of our true worship and not worship itself. True worship is obedience to God. It's what we are willing to sacrifice. Although Abraham knows what God is requiring, he mentions in Genesis 22:5 that he and his son would go to worship and that BOTH of them would return. This speaks that our worship is a manifestation of our total trust in God. It is the acknowledgement that we don't always understand God's mind, but we can always trust God's heart. Understanding God is not a prerequisite of worship. A God that I can totally comprehend with my finite mind is not one worth worshipping. As a believer we can know God and forever learn Him. The parts of Him I don't understand doesn't make me doubt Him, but it causes me to worship him. If you are familiar with this passage about Abraham and Isaac, you know that God interrupts Abraham before he sacrifices his son. It was a test of his faith and devotion. At that moment the Angel of the Lord tells him, "now I know you fear God." Many biblical scholars would argue that this angel is actually God himself or the son of God in an angelic/human form. But the question arises in me, did God have to test Abraham to know Abraham? God put him through all of that just to say, now I know that you fear me. I believe that God is omniscient, meaning all knowing. There is nothing that the God who is eternal does not know. But I believe that all-knowing God places moments in time just to give us the opportunity to choose him. Worship is choosing GOD daily. When we decide to worship, we are lifting His name and His agenda above all else.

One hot evening in India I was leaving a small village called Syrupet with Pastor Silvi Kothopally. He was taking me back to the large bustling city of Hyderabad. It was a two-hour drive on a very narrow but heavily traffic congested road. We decided to stop by a simple roadside store to get some refreshments. While sitting on this bench a little boy came to me speaking Telugu, the local dialect. He was holding a little box in his hand with a little figure in the center. I didn't understand his language, but he kept pointing at the figure on the inside of the box. Finally, the translator informed me that the little boy was asking me to give an offering to his god. I then asked where was this god and the translator pointed toward the little figure in the box. In that moment I sat with gratitude when I considered my God. He had to carry his god, but the God I worship carries me.

Day Sixteen
Keep Still

Growing up as a hyper kid, "keep still" were words of command that I heard on a regular basis. I had a very close relationship with my mother's sister growing up. We call her Aunt Peggy. She's like a second mom to me. She's always been a jack of all trades with many talents. When we were younger, she picked up the hobby of cutting hair. My cousins and I became her guinea pigs. Her clippers were not always the softest upon our heads in her practice stage. She would try to cut my hair and I would squirm in the chair as she would forcefully try to hold my head still so she could do her work. I sometimes see that image with us and God. There are times when He's working on our heads, but often we don't trust His hands.

The children of Israel had been delivered from Egypt after centuries of slavery. Very quickly they found themselves facing the Red Sea with their enemies approaching them from behind. Fear began to take over the newly freed Israelites and they began to murmur against their God-given leader Moses. In Exodus 14:13 Moses said, "Fear ye not, stand still, and see the salvation of the Lord, which he will show to you today." The bible tells us that Moses held up his rod and the Israelites crossed over on dry ground and their enemies drowned behind them. If they had ran back from God, they would've run into the hands of their enemies. Running ahead, they would have drowned in the Red Sea. Standing still, however, gave them a front seat to a miracle. It's innate in us to try to fix things and work things out. We have control issues, but life will bring you situations that you have no power over.

Trying to work things out can sometimes make things worse. Some people look at being still as a lack of concern. But for others, it's an image of total trust. When I was around nine years old, my family and I rode the church bus to another city for an event. After the church event, myself along with my mother and grandmother were some of the first people back on the bus. People began to board the bus one by one when all of sudden someone accidentally pushed against the gear shift of the old bus. The bus started rolling backwards down the hill. People began to scream, and I tried to run down the aisle of the bus, but my mother and grandmother held on to me and sat still. I can still see and hear this moment vividly in my head. Fortunately, one of the deacons, Charlie Johnson miraculously made his way to the front of the bus and stopped it. Being still in that moment was not easy. However, if I was allowed to jump in the aisle, I would have obstructed Charlie's path to the front of the bus. In our attempt to help God we often hinder Him. I know it sounds contradictory, but an omnipotent God in all of the vastness of His power is in some ways limited in our lives to what we will allow Him to do. I recall the times when we were children and when those summer storms would come; my grandmother would tell us to be quiet and keep still because God was doing His work. This was teaching me at an early age that stillness was reverencing the power of God and giving Him access to work in our lives.

Don't allow the rat race of this life make you go ahead of God's timing. Keep still until you receive divine direction. Philippians 4:6 says, "Do not be anxious about anything, but in every situation, by prayer and petition, with thanksgiving, present your requests to God." Anything God has for you doesn't have to be rushed or forced. God is an eternal being that operates in time. There are circumstances in life where you will find yourself blocked in like those Israelites in Exodus. During those times, your assignment will be to simply keep still. At times this posture will be easier said than done. For many this act of obedience will save us from destruction. In Psalm 46:10 the Lord says, "Be Still and Know that I am God. This tells me that God is revealed in our stillness. Moses knows this truth very well. The reason Moses experienced God in the burning bush is because he was still long enough to notice that the bush was not being consumed.

Maybe today's entry seems like it doesn't belong in this devotional book. Keep Going implies movement. Keeping Still suggests that one is stagnant, stuck, or immobile. Although I understand that perspective, I beg to differ. Due to my itinerant schedule, most of my nights are spent in hotel rooms. Sometimes it's a different hotel each night. Due to this consistently nomadic lifestyle, sometimes I go to the wrong hotel room trying to use my key from the night before. Many times, when the elevator door opens, I automatically walk off. These elevator experiences have taught me some valuable lessons:

1). Just because the door opens it doesn't mean it's your turn to get off. Every opportunity is not a divine door.

2). The decorations and furniture may look the same, but it's not your floor. Make sure you're not so distracted that you let familiarity mislead you.

3). Don't move out just because everyone else is moving. Wait for your floor.

4). You may be in it longer because you're going higher.

5). My last lesson learned from a hotel elevator is the fact that you can still move while being still.

Read this prayer aloud:
Father help me to wait for you and let you be God. I now relinquish my desire to control my own life and the situations around me. I don't trust myself to choose for myself. Lord daily teach me how to trust you. Show yourself strong in my life, in Jesus name.

Day Seventeen
Keep Loving

Love is beautiful. In my lifetime, I've been a recipient and a distributor of it. However, I haven't always received it from the people that I gave it to. It's easier to be disappointed by a stranger because without a relationship there's no real expectations. But the greatest hurt someone can ever endure is one that has been inflicted upon them by an individual they genuinely love. STOP regretting ever loving them. You gave them love. What they did with it is a reflection of them, but you must remember how you loved them is a reflection of you. While we were yet sinners, Christ died for us. Someone would call that crazy, but that's God's kind of love. If love is God, that means love is multi-dimensional. Love is not just about receiving; love is also refraining. Love is both celebrating and correcting.

I met a girl in college who I fell for. The only problem was that she had a boyfriend, and an even bigger problem was that he was a big football player. I digress. This girl and I were friends, and the more time I spent with her, the more my feelings grew. Eventually, her relationship with the football player dissolved, so I moved in. This turned into many years of back and forth, break ups and reunions, until we called it quits. We loved each other. A lot of things happened over the years, but those problems didn't change the fact that what we felt was real. I don't regret loving. As I reflect now, I know I loved her, but maybe I loved the idea of her more than I loved her. We are still in each other's lives today, and we still love each other. That love has a different expectation, but it's still love.

You may ask yourself, "How can I still love after hurt, rejection, and disappointment?" It's because I believe we have romanticized love to the point that it has lost all of its sobriety. If all of our love stories were made by Disney, every curse of lovesickness would be broken, and every beast would be turned into a gentleman with true love's kiss. But these kinds of fairy tales carry little resemblance to the love we should seek in hurt and happiness, rejection and rejuvenation, disappointment and delight.

I don't believe we should fall in love like Disney characters; I think we should stand up in it like as if we were accepting a call of duty or responsibility. You see, love comes with feelings, passions, and desires, but it ultimately becomes a decision. We make a decision to love. When we read 1 Corinthians 13, we hear that love is kind, long-suffering, self-sacrificial. You won't always feel like doing those things, but you can always make a decision to do those things.

I realized that she really does love me. I know she does, because she did not accept my hand in marriage. Ultimately, she let me go, but even that's love.

So, maybe your expectation of love has been disappointed or altered, leaving you hurt and emotionally bruised. Maybe these disappointments have made you decide that you will never be hurt that way again. Maybe you have started putting precautionary measures in place to protect your heart. Maybe there is an imaginary moat between you and others. Maybe you have even successfully locked everyone out without realizing that you have actually locked yourself in.

In your attempt to protect yourself from hurt, you will also protect yourself from love. Love comes with a price, but it also comes with an unmatched treasure, so keep loving.

Day Eighteen
Keep Praising

My life is an example to many,
because you have been my strength and protection.
That is why I can never stop praising you;
I declare your glory all day long.

Psalm 71:7-8

Have you ever worked with someone and noticed that they have always found something to complain about? It makes you wonder, if they were in charge of everything, would they complain about themselves? You can find it hard to encourage someone who doesn't want to be encouraged. You will quickly discover that it's not the elements that are around them that makes them pessimistic, but it's something within them. You must be careful not to let their negativity contaminate your spirit. We could all find something to complain about, but the truth is there are no positive benefits to it. Complaining produces tension, built up frustration, depression, increased confusion and division. Complaining in itself is not a solution. As a matter of fact, some people who complain have no desire to find a solution. Their disgruntled position has become their cloak or garment.

There's an alternative position to complaining, that's called praise. To praise something or someone means to speak highly, express admiration, or to pay tribute. The culture of praise produces many positive benefits. It attracts people to you. It's difficult to work for or with someone who never acknowledges an accomplishment or improvement. We can be so focused on strategizing, building, and implementing that we fail to praise the people around us and even God for what has already been accomplished. Just as we find things to complain about, we can easily find something to praise about.

Finally, brethren, whatsoever things are true, whatsoever things are honest, whatsoever things are just, whatsoever things are pure, whatsoever things are lovely, whatsoever things are of good report; if there be any virtue, and if there be any praise, think on these things.

Today work on praising your students, co-workers, spouse, and your children. You would be surprised what it will do for them when they receive a positive text from you. You will also discover their value to your life, ministry, company etc. We sometimes don't realize all someone does until we stop and evaluate. Maybe the dishes are still in the sink from last night, but don't forget about the eight baskets of laundry that are now cleaned and folded. Start praising.

The Collection of Psalms admonishes us throughout its pages to praise God. Just as people are attracted to us when we praise them, this happens even more with God. Psalm 22:3 says "But thou art holy, O thou that inhabitest the praises of Israel." When we speak well of God, you can actually feel His tangible presence. I believe that every prayer should begin in praise. Not starting a prayer in praise is almost like shouting out our demands at God from another room in the house. Praise should never be used as an attempt to manipulate God, but true praise should be about honoring Him. When we praise God, not only does God come down in the midst of it, but God comes down with Himself as Himself. God is love, joy, peace, wholeness, healing, and strength; this is what we experience when we praise Him.

I will bless the Lord at all times: his praise shall continually be in my mouth.
My soul shall make her boast in the Lord: the humble shall hear thereof, and be glad.
O magnify the Lord with me, and let us exalt his name together.
Psalm 34:1-3

One day a woman told me after visiting my church that she noticed that all of the people in our worship service started dancing at the same time; implying as though it was premeditated. She was surprised when I agreed with her. I shared with her that praise is a volunteering intentional act. If God made us do it, it wouldn't be praise. It's what makes us different than all the other creation, we get to decide to praise him. I'm not saying everyone should dance; for I understand that praise is universal. But, many forms or styles of praise is cultural. I am saying that you have to be intentional.

Create your own culture of praise. Start the day praising God for 10 things that make you grateful. Play praise music on your way to work and sing along to it. Be prepared to share a praise report with someone at your job concerning the goodness of the LORD. David said, "I will bless the LORD at all times." All times is not in reference to the different hours in a 24- hour day. Instead, it refers to the different times of your life. Your praise should never be predicated on your situation, it should always be reflective of your GOD. In Psalm 71:7, the psalmist said my life is an example to many because of God's strength and protection. There will be days when there is no song that can carry the lyrics of your heartbeat towards God. Your legs won't have the strength to dance, but in those moments, the fact that you even exist will be praise to GOD. Keep Praising.

Day Nineteen
Keep Growing

Recently, I was asked to accompany my ten-year-old nephew to his basketball banquet. It was close to the end of the season, and I was pretty familiar with this sort of event when they acknowledge the accomplishments of the players. We sat through the banquet filled with fruit punch and pizza boxes-the age appropriate menu. After the coach finished a short speech sharing his sentiments about the kids' characters and personality traits, he went on to distribute a trophy to each child. All of the parents and guardians clapped with great enthusiasm after each child's name was called.

My nephew is very smart and witty. He's also a cool kid. He was sitting with all of his friends at this banquet. Of course, I embarrassed him when they called his name. The coach said, "Kylon Smith." I then jumped up out of my seat wearing my three-piece suit amongst a group of casually-dressed people and cheered as if he had made a touchdown on the football field. He commenced to walk in shame as he received his modest plastic trophy.

During the car ride home, I attempted to start up a conversation with my niece and nephew. I began to share with my nephew about how proud I was of him and his team's accomplishments that year. Then, with a cunning smirk and the palms of his hands lifted, he said to me, "But we didn't win any games." With bewilderment I asked him to repeat his statement. It was true; he informed me that during the entire season, his team had lost every single game. I wondered what the trophies and banquet were all about.

In our society, we give out trophies simply for showing up and doing what's required- even if we don't actually accomplish or excel in anything. I understand the perspective of those who say that we should give children trophies to build their self-esteem, but I wonder, too, if there is a damaging side effect of it. This perspective may in large help continue to breed a culture of entitlement, not one of intentional growth. This type of ideology causes people to feel as though they did their employer a favor by merely showing up- even

64

if they don't produce anything. This causes a generation to make attendance synonymous with achievement.

In this way, lowering the bar actually hinders growth. No one has ever achieved greatness from a seat of comfort. The eagle's ability to fly comes from the pricking of the nest. The bodybuilder increases muscle mass by choosing the weights that cause resistance. As much as I hate taking tests, they often assess far we've grown from the last point of examination.

Do you remember when you were learning to walk? Every time you got close to a steady hand, your parent would then step back. It can seem like a frustrating game from a small baby's perspective, but the goal is to get the timid, tottering child to go further than before. This process is called growth.

God himself does this with us, His children. God will sometimes pull back from us so that we will seek after Him. If you're not growing, you're not moving. If you're not moving, you're stuck. If you never get past the same two steps or if you pick up the same weights over and over again, you don't need a trophy; you need a challenge. There are times when we look at challenges as an opportunity to retreat or run, but we need to look at challenges as opportunities to grow. We also like to stay in the place of our mastery. After all, no one likes to feel inadequate or insufficient. But, yet and still, outside of our place of mastery, there's room to grow-which is a sign of life. If you're not growing, then you're dying.

We should find relationships that push us to grow. Don't allow people to hold you to the place where you started. Sometimes people will try to hinder your growth because your growth exposes their stagnancy. Other times, you will become complacent because you're comparing yourself to other complacent people. While I'm not advising you to abandon all of your past friendships, I am telling you that growth changes relationship dynamics. This is why it's especially important for a couple to grow together. For example, if one pursues growth alone in the area of finances, education, or even spirituality, it will automatically cause friction. This friction will either encourage growth together or create a barrier.

65

Paul said in 1 Corinthians 13:11, "When I was a child, I spoke as a child, I understood as a child, I thought as a child: but when I became a man, I put away childish things. There are things that you have no control over. You can't control what people say about you or how they treat you. You know you have grown when the behavior of others doesn't affect you the same way it would have years or even weeks ago. Many of us know we have grown when we don't respond to people and situations like we used to in our past. When you stand at a different height, you gain a different vantage point. You just have to keep growing to get there.

I grew up in the beautiful Gretna, Virginia. I call it beautiful not because of its landscape but because of the people. I've learned over the years that it's not where you are that makes a place special. Rather, it's who you're with. The population in the whole town of Gretna is made up of about only 1,300 people. In Gretna, our main grocery store was called Amos Fine Foods; it was named after the Amos family that ran it. Our popular fast food spot was Jack's, which didn't have a drive-thru, but you could walk right up to the window and get the best hotdogs in your life. The local pharmacy was not a part of a national chain; it was called Gretna Drug Store. Growing up, I used to quote the town's motto that was put on the signs and banners. The sign read, "Welcome to Gretna, Virginia… Ain't No Big Thing But It's Growing!"

This motto reflected our southern dialect and charm, and it's still used today. A lot of things are the same now, but a lot of things have changed in Gretna since I was a boy. There's still Jack's, but we also have a Food Lion grocery store among other national chains and franchises. Over the years, Gretna hasn't seen a huge population boom or even a lot of annexed property. But I've seen a change in the infrastructure of the town. My little town doesn't have a Broadway Theatre, but it has fostered the Gretna Little Theatre-- allowed local talent to showcase and perform plays. Gretna is not New York City, and I'm not comparing it to them, but it's growing. Your growth can not be compared to that of someone else. Instead of comparing yourself to someone else's growth, compare yourself to the person you were yesterday.

The life of Isaac in the Book of Genesis is filled with great dynamics. Every time he tried to open the wells that his father dug, he was met with great contention. No matter where he went, he was consistently met with great challenges, but it didn't stop his growth. There is one scripture that speaks of the life Isaac in his season of great opposition. Genesis 26:13 says, "And the man waxed great, and went forward, and grew until he became very great."

Today, determine to be like Isaac. Be great and keep growing.

Day Twenty
Keep Living

I often wonder what people see when they see me. I guess it will depend on who you ask and which day of the week you ask. On paper I think my life looks pretty good. I'm well-traveled and I've had some major accomplishments. I say these things humbly because anything bad about me is all me, but anything good about me is all God. If you Google my biography and resume, it looks pretty impressive, but I feel like it's misleading and I'm not alone in my assessment. There are many that embellish their resume and airbrush their headshots to present the best image of themselves. This method of polishing one's presentation or twisting one's background for a desired employment opportunity is not what I'm referencing. Everything in my bio is accurate and nothing has been embellished, but yet I still feel it's misleading. It's misleading because it attempts to give you a picture of who I am totally based upon my accomplishments. Our biographical sketch seeks to highlight our greatest moments and victories. It paints a picture of our mountain top experiences where we stood at the peak taking selfies, but it often fails to show the low place that we sometimes experienced directly afterward. That's my truth.

I used to question what would drive someone to the point where they didn't want to live anymore. As I've grown older, I've been able to understand why someone would think this way. My vocation as a pastor has given me a front row seat to a myriad of reasons why someone would want to stop living. Someone can be suffering from a terminal health issue that has rendered an undesired quality of life. An individual can be suffering from the loss of a loved one, and the grief is too much to bear. A person can feel like giving up once they have lost their company, home or whatever they worked hard to build and starting over seems impossible. There are also moments when a person has experienced a failure or embarrassment and they feel the public shame is too much to psychologically handle. These moments can put an individual in the seat of hopelessness.

There have been many skeptics and atheists over the years that have brought into question the authenticity of the Bible. Some have minimized its worth to that of Greek mythology. I believe the Bible is an accurate, historical, and vivid account of the people and events it records. One argument against my confidence in the scriptures is the fact that it was written by men. This claim only fuels my faith. Why would someone make up a story and not portray themselves as the hero of that story? Why would you display your most intimate secrets and flaws in writing? Why would you use words to paint yourself as a weak individual? You would do these things only if you were committed to telling the truth. It's because of the transparency of their lives upon the pages of the scripture that causes me to connect in this modern day to an ancient text. When I get to Heaven, I want to thank Jesus for keeping his scars for the sake of my faith. I want to thank Rahab the prostitute for showing up in the genealogy of Jesus. Her story proves to me that your past lifestyle doesn't have to determine your future destiny. Lastly, I want to thank Elijah for showing me that you can be anointed, called, chosen, gifted, and still struggle with depression. Elijah was a master prophet. I refer to him as a master prophet because he led a school of prophets. He was one of the most noted prophets of all scriptures. From the mouth of Elijah, the rain would cease; and he would then speak again, and the rain would fall. The Spirit of God would come upon him and he could outrun men on horseback. One of his most iconic moments is his stance on Mount Carmel. There on the top of the mountain was a showdown, as if it were some sort of contest. It was the prophet Elijah up against 400 prophets of Baal. Both sides claimed to be worshippers of the right deity. They resolved that whichever god answered by fire, would be declared the true god. The prophets of Baal cut themselves and cried out loud, but there was no fire. Elijah set up an altar, poured water, and called out to his God and GOD answered by fire. On that day the false prophets were slain, Elijah was declared victorious, and God was magnified in the eyes of the people. Shortly after, Elijah got a message from the evil queen Jezebel threatening that she was going to kill him. How does the most powerful prophet in the land respond? He runs. The same prophet that stood boldly upon the mountain has now descended emotionally to the valley. Not only does he run, but also, he sends his servant away. This is someone who was there to assist him, but in a moment of anxiety he sends help away. Ecclesiastes 4:9 says that "two are better than one," but when we go through difficult times in our lives, sometimes our first instinct or response is to isolate ourselves. During these times many of us stop answering phone calls, stop attending church, leave the family group chat, or just withdraw from any social interaction. You can't do hard times alone. We very quickly shut down from an emotional perspective- assuming that no one understands our unique situation. Remember that God will bring people into your life who do not need to understand the details of your dilemma in order to walk with you through it. Elijah is left alone, and he begins to pray. His prayer is not elaborate but it's really simple, "let me die." The man who experienced victory on the mountain now feels that it would be better if he weren't living. What would cause Elijah to pray this? Elijah is tired. He stands for God consistently and sometimes he stands alone. He's strong, but even strong people need strength.

Many of us feel we can identify with Elijah. We feel that we never have time to recover before we are faced with another challenge, problem, or situation. Although Elijah's last encounter was a success, we must realize that even great accomplishments will exert one's emotional, spiritual, and physical energy. When the woman touched the hem of Jesus' garment, He asked who touched Him after feeling virtue leave out of His body. When we consistently serve, counsel and take care of others, there is something that is being extracted from us. Imagine as soon as you have prayed down fire from Heaven; slayed the false prophets; and now you're faced with another threat. Elijah wanted a break. He didn't feel like fighting anymore. There are those who love a good quarrel. However, there are those of us who deal with challenges so frequently that they would actually welcome and enjoy the days of nothingness. I'm referring to the days where there's no trauma, drama, or scores to settle. Jezebel's present threat tried to fog Elijah's memory. Don't allow your present challenge to make you forget your past victory. We want to die and quit in these moments because we feel that we don't have any strength to fight. Depression makes you feel like you're drowning; and every time you come up to the surface for air, something else pushes you right back down.

When you're dealing with depression, it's an ongoing fight. You have to fight to get out of bed, fight to get dressed, fight to appear happy, and fight just to be present for the people you love. Remember, the same God who is on the mountain is the same God who is in the valley.

"If I go up to the heavens, you are there; if I make my bed in the depths, you are there" (Psalm 139:8).

Elijah goes to sleep under a juniper tree and is awakened by the touch of an angel. Imagine, he has run from Jezebel and has even distanced himself from his servant, but he still was able to experience a touch from the angel. No matter how distant you may feel, you're not so far that God can't reach you. The angel instructs him to eat the food that's already cooked and to drink the water that's prepared. After Elijah ate, he then went back to sleep. The angel woke him a second time and told him to eat. Ironically, Elijah prays for death but instead gets food. Throughout the scripture, we see Elijah pray for others, but we never see him pray for himself. Consider this, a chef doesn't get full off of the food he cooks. He gets full off the food he eats. If you ever plan to regain your strength, you must eat. Matthew 4:4 says, "But he answered and said, It is written, Man shall not live by bread alone, but by every word that proceedeth out of the mouth of God." The word of God is a meal that has already been prepared. Rise and eat. When you're in a low place, you must place yourself in an environment that feeds you. You may even have to create this type of environment yourself.

The second time the angel instructed him to eat was because the journey ahead of him was too much. It seems like God totally ignored Elijah's resignation. I believe in these types of moments. God remembers the surrender of our hearts when the rationale of our minds has retreated, and our faith has escaped us. When people want to die it's because they can't see past the moment they are in. The angel starts to inform the prophet that there is a king he must coronate and another prophet that he must anoint. If God ever gives you information concerning your tomorrow, it is a strong indication that you won't die today. If there is a new king and a young prophet waiting on Elijah, this means his life and purpose is bigger than he.

71

In the moments we want to stop living, we must remember that someone's destiny is tied to our survival.

As a man of faith, I've experienced some low moments that made me want to die. I was a young pastor full of energy and passion. My desire was to be everything that everyone wanted me to be. When I look back at those moments, I realize how unhealthy that desire really was. I was doing a lot of good things, but because I failed to maintain my own spiritual and emotional health, I began to operate out of my own ability and not from God's spirit. I hit rock bottom. Things that I once would get over rather quickly began to weigh me down. The voices of my critics were being amplified in my ears. Small challenges were being magnified in my mind. My grandfather who raised me died in my home. I experienced some leaders leave the church I pastored. My courting relationship came to a halt. Instead of resisting temptation, I started yielding to temptation. This gave me more of a reason why I should just quit. The responsibilities were making me feel claustrophobic and I just didn't want to hurt anymore. On this particular Sunday I called my assistant pastor and his wife in my office. I shared with them where I was spiritually and mentally. I informed them that when I left the church on that day, I wasn't sure if I would return but for them to promise me, they would continue the work. I went home, got in bed, and cried. I cried so long that I was left with the sound of crying without any tears left to shed. I was too sober to commit suicide, but I prayed selfishly for God to take me in my sleep. When I woke up there was a couple from my church in my room. These people had been with me from the beginning of my pastoral ministry. The husband was on the right side of my bed and the wife was on the left. Just as Elijah had angels that came to feed him; I had Ted and Sonya. They stayed by me and prayed for me. They didn't weigh me down with a lot of questions. They kept rehearsing the testimonies of days past and reminding me of the journey ahead. Their words brought life back to my spirit. Life is a precious gift, but the maintenance of it is often painful. This means pain is a part of the gift. It's the depths of the valleys that gives the mountains their height. Every day given to you is an indication from the Lord that there is purpose left in you. You may be left with fragments and miscellaneous pieces that don't seem to have a pattern or fit. Keep living. God has a way of making sense out of the chaos of our lives. There is a Baptist hymn that I often hum that speaks to me:

We are often tossed and driven
On the restless sea of time
Somber skies and howling tempests
Oft' succeed a bright sunshine.
In that land of perfect day,
When the mists have rolled away,
We will understand it better by and by.

Day Twenty-One
Keep Pedaling

When I was around 10 years old, my grandmother sent me on an errand down the street, to a nearby neighbor's house. I was very willing because I was always looking for an opportunity to ride my bike beyond the perimeters of our yard. When I arrived at the neighbor's house, she already had the items placed in a used plastic grocery bag. I headed back home with the bag hanging from my bicycle handle. Then the dog came. I have always had a fear of dogs. I don't know the reason behind this fear, but if it wasn't our family dog, I didn't trust it. On this particular day, my worst fears came alive when, a black dog came out of nowhere chasing behind my bike. I was frantic and, in that moment, I made an irrational decision. I jumped off of the bike and ran. I came home with no bag and one shoe. Of course, I had a lot of explaining to do. My grandmother was and still is a very warm, but strong, southern, African American woman. In response to my speech about the dog, she made me go back up the street and confiscate the bag of items, my bike and my shoe. I found all of the items there on the side of the street untouched with my bike. It seemed that the dog wasn't after the items, he was just after me. When I returned home once again my grandmother asked me a simple yet profound question. She asked, "Why did you jump off the bike?" She explained to me that I had a better chance of getting away from the dog if I would have kept pedaling.

We all have fears that serve as opposing enemies to our faith. There are times when we feel as though we are over certain fears until we are actually faced with them. That day I was riding the bike, so I wasn't expecting a dog. This is the way life goes. You can be riding along and enjoying the season you're in; when all of a sudden you are faced with your worst fear. Fear can make you forget what you know. It will paralyze you and cause you to make irrational decisions. When you find yourself in these circumstances, you have to speak what you know to be true. You have to recall the Word of God back to yourself.

This I recall to my mind, therefore have, I hope.
It is of the Lord's mercies that we are not consumed, because his
compassions fail not.
They are new every morning: great is thy faithfulness.

Lamentations 3:21-23

Don't focus on your fears, instead choose to focus on God's
faithfulness. When you are in the midst of a challenge, this may
seem difficult. But you must remind yourself that the challenge is
simply a threat. The threats of the enemy will make you feel that
you are losing your mind. Fear is more than an emotion, it's an evil
spirit. This spirit will attack your cognitive skills and your ability to
thoroughly process a proper reaction.

For God hath not given us the spirit of fear; but of power, and of
love, and of a sound mind.
2 Timothy 1:7

God is in control. This fact does not change at the arrival of your
recent adversity. When John sees Jesus in heaven, Jesus is not
pacing back and forth. He is not nervous or panicking. He is found
seated on the throne. The story of Job reminds us that as believers,
there is nothing that we are faced with that didn't first go by God.
He knew the dog was coming. God knew about the medical
diagnosis, the accident, the financial challenge, and the family
issues. Although these things may have taken you off guard, He was
already aware.

My grandmother reminded me that I had a better chance of getting
away from the dog on the bicycle. Fear makes you jump off of what
God has given you to successfully overcome what's pursuing you.
Encounters of great fear and despair will cause you to jump off of
your bike. Your bike may be the people around you. In your
survival mode, you risk severing divine relationships that are
designed to strengthen you. For example, you may even leave a
church that was feeding you. Your fear will cause you to pull away
from your family that was helping you. In Psalm 116, David said, "I
said in my haste, all men are liars." In despair David spoke
prematurely and resolved that every person is a liar. We know that

75

this statement is not true. But David's despair caused him to make a broad judgement based off of a specific experience. In essence, he made an irrational or thoughtless statement out of fear and despair. He erroneously concluded to give up on the human race as a whole- a people incapable of being honest and truthful.

Stay on the bike. My little used bike may not have been perfect, but God used it to get me home. The dog was never after my stuff, he was after me. He was just trying to get me to move from his territory. This was a sobering revelation. I noticed that after I dropped the items and ran out of his territory, he gave up the pursuit. Your greatest fears may be surfacing because you are infiltrating the enemies' territory. If you've ever jumped off of what God gave you out of fear; go back, recover your stuff, get back on the bike, and keep pedaling.

And the Lord said, Simon, Simon, behold, Satan hath desired to have you, that he may sift you as wheat:

But I have prayed for thee, that thy faith fail not: and when thou art converted, strengthen thy brethren.

Luke 22:31-32

Day Twenty-Two
Keep Breathing

There are moments in life that will take your breath away. When we hear about these moments, we often think of romantic moments, ecstatic surprises, or even intense workouts. But there are also moments in life that will literally make you feel that you cannot breathe. There's an old African American expression I remember hearing when I was growing up in the rural south. "You done went and got the wind knocked right outta ya!" This expression refers to those moments when you received news or had an unexpected, tragic, and traumatic experience.

All it takes is one text message, one phone call, one email, or even one knock on the door to shift your entire life completely.

In ministry counseling, we are always taught not to get too emotionally tied to a client or parishioner. This would begin to alter our ability to serve or do ministry. Over the years, I've heard a myriad of stories and confessions, and I've never acted or appeared shocked after hearing them. I will be taking most of those counseling sessions to my grave. I will also lose some to my lack of memory. However, there are some moments that have been seared in my memory for a lifetime, as a result of their significant emotional impact. One story in particular that I will share, with permission, is about the day I received a call from a man that I will call Calvin. He called on the eve of his forty sixth birthday. As he called, I could hear tears and confusion in his voice. Calvin shared with me that his teenage son had shared a shocking Facebook message. This message revealed that the father who raised Calvin was not his biological father. Calvin, of course, did not take this news seriously because he had a close relationship with his father. Surely, he wasn't going to take the word of some stranger on Facebook. It wasn't until Calvin's son showed him a photo of another man shown in the message. This is when the messenger's claim made things all too real-implicating that this message could possibly be true. Calvin lost his breath. When Calvin saw the photo, there was not just a strong resemblance, but Calvin noticed a complete reflection. Everything he thought he knew came into question at that moment. Moving forward to today, Calvin, who found out that his dad wasn't his biological father, got a chance to meet his birth father. I had the privilege of being there to witness that reunion. A moment that first took his breath away ended up giving him a second wind. He now has an extended of family of siblings he didn't know he had.

We all have our own recollection of unexpected and traumatic experiences. Our entire worlds are changed beyond what we could ever imagine. For example, imagine when someone learns that their spouse has been unfaithful. For someone else, a diligent employee's world comes crashing down when they arrive at their job to find out they no longer have a position. Others freeze at the loss of a child through a tragic accident. In those moments, we stop breathing.

What do you do when life takes your breath away? You stop, you center yourself, you focus, and then you breathe again. Of course, doing this is easier said than done. Although these instructions are listed as easy steps, they are considered a process and a journey. After following those steps, you will notice the need to go back to the beginning and begin again.

You may ask what to focus on now that I have advised you to focus and breathe again. In these moments when your emotional, spiritual, and even physical equilibrium is completely off, choose to focus on something that is stable. Remind yourself of what you know to be real. Choosing to focus on something that is stable.

"Whatsoever is true, whatever things are noble, whatever things are just, whatever things are pure, whatever things are lovely, whatever things are of good report, if there is any virtue, and if there be any praise, think on these things."

Philippians 4:8

This gives you reassurance and security in the midst of a life altering experience. In that moment, you will be completely bombarded with the notion that everything has changed. In these moments, learn to take a deep breath and see what hasn't shifted. Before you lost your breath, you were loved by God. And you still are. That fact hasn't changed. When you find yourself gasping for air, remember that you are loved.

The Bible says that Jesus told the disciples, "Let us go over to the other side." Once the disciples got into the boat, a storm arose. The disciples began panicking. However, Jesus was in the bottom of the boat asleep.

In the same manner, Jesus slept in a storm because there was no storm in Him. The disciples failed to remember what He said. Storms will attempt to make you forget the instructions you received at the beginning of your journey. The instructions from Jesus said, "Let's go over to the other side." Jesus had spoken that they were going over to the other side. Despite the storm we may encounter, we *will* make it to the other side. Jesus said that He gives peace. More specifically, He gives *His* peace--the kind of peace that can settle your spirit and help you breathe in the middle of anything. The bible also records Peter being locked up in prison and sleep. Through this, Peter shows us that when you have God's peace, in the midst of being locked in a panicking situation, it does not mean that you are locked out of God's presence.

Looking back, in retrospect, I didn't realize that I suffered from anxiety. I'm a motivator, a coach, a preacher, and I consider myself as someone who has a lot of faith. But I still found myself suffering from anxiety. Anxiety is a feeling of worry, nervousness, and unease. Typically, one experiences bouts of anxiety as it relates to an impending event or something with an unknown outcome. For a long time, I was embarrassed to even acknowledge my anxiety. As a result, I did not speak about this struggle and found myself suffering silently. There are a few reasons why I felt I couldn't share about my anxiety. Foremost, it was because I am a man. Social norms tell us that men are not afraid. And if they are, they are not to express that they were afraid. Also, I'm a Pentecostal preacher, which implies that I have a great depth of spiritual revelation regarding the Holy Scriptures and the mysteries of God. I speak different dialects of heavenly languages (better known as speaking in tongues). My denominational affiliation implies that I believe in the casting out of demons.

With that background, you would understand why I wasn't quick to raise my hand and acknowledge my struggle with anxiety. I felt my acknowledgement would make me look like an imposter. As a matter of fact, I felt like one-an imposter. After all, if I have all of this faith, power, and strength, why I would suffer from anxiety? To me, my declaration of faith combined with my experiences with anxiety sounds like a contradiction. How could I confess such faith and still suffer from anxiety? This sounded like a contradiction to me. I could identify with the disciples who said, "Lord, I believe, but help thou my unbelief." But then, I realized that maybe I didn't have to wait for all my fear to be gone before I could truly believe. Maybe I didn't have to wait for all my moments of feeling weak to dissipate before I could be strong.

That's because it's not faith *outside* of doubt. Consider, it's faith *in the midst of* doubt. When I realized this truth, I was able to stand in power and acknowledge my hardships with anxiety. I understand now, more than ever, that it takes a strong person to suffer while still yet believing and trusting. We will, however, revisit the ability to keep believing in a separate chapter.

If you are familiar with my ministry, you will know that my work requires me to travel around the world. I travel so often that I've climbed to premier client status in Hilton properties and I've racked up many airline miles. However, many people didn't know, that as I was traveling around the world, I was afraid of flying. My fear of flying was so intense, that each night before a flight, I found myself not being able to sleep. I don't know if it was my constant diet of watching tragic news feeds on television or my subconscious being aware of my inability to control the environment. But anxiety had nearly ruined my love affair with being a world traveler. I was desperate to overcome this hindrance. Flying was an essential tool in being able to accomplish my goals and fulfill my purpose. As an extreme, I even entertained the idea of taking medication. However, all of the medicine prescribed for anxiety had the potential of making me drowsy as a side effect. This would render me unable to reach my full potential when I landed since I usually was heading to a speaking engagement. After doing some research, and listening to the reoccurring advice from professionals, I learned that taking deep breaths lessens the feeling of anxiety. I don't know what I was looking for as I researched this, but this solution seemed very anticlimactic to me. As soon as we start having feelings of anxiety, the first thing that is affected is our breathing pattern. With this understanding, when we breathe, we find it easier to trust.

Man was just an empty mannequin or shell until God breathed into him. Every moment of anxiety is robbing you of the life that God has given you. You risk being able to fully enjoy the experience of life. The bible instructs us to be anxious for nothing. I had settled for flying in fear and stress. Oftentimes, I arrived at my location exhausted because I was not trusting. I was not trusting and as a result, I put myself at risk of not enjoying the experience or my time spent at a certain location. I was fearing something that may or may not ever happen. I decided that this was not the way I wanted to live. According to Jesus' teachings, you can't add height to yourself or change the outcome, if you spend so much time worrying.

You may ask me how I overcame and experienced deliverance regarding this area of anxiety. My first step was to make a decision. Whatever you struggle with in life, you must make a decision regarding the struggle. Choose to decide where you stand regarding that particular struggle. Whatever the struggle is; whether your struggle is regarding drugs, alcohol, sex, or anxiety, you must choose to make a decision about it. What is your posture regarding the struggle? Where do you stand and what are your beliefs regarding a certain struggle? Do you want this struggle to hinder you? You must decide if this struggle is something you desire to overcome. The next step is to take authority. It's one thing for you to have a struggle, but it's another thing when that struggle has you. You have to speak out loud to further increase your ability to trust. There were times when I was on the plane and would experience turbulence. I would whisper to myself and say, "You are ok." Be encouraged in knowing that you always make it, God has you! You may not be able to change the way you feel, but you are able to change what you say. When I see the Almighty God, I don't see Him pacing back and forth with His Hands wringing with sweat. He's seated on the throne. He's not anxious, and He's not nervous. He has everything in control. Trust in that. Trust in Him.

In case you're wondering about my fear of flying, just know that I'm still flying every week. Keep Breathing.

Day Twenty-Three
Keep Marching

The Civil Rights Movement in America is full of famously named and unnamed heroes alike. The courage of these individuals inspire us in America and others around the world. What courage they possessed! They were fighting for every human being to be treated fairly and given equal opportunities- regardless of the color of their skin or socio-economic status. Individuals played a diverse number of roles in these righteous fights. There were some who donated their legal services to representing those who chose to challenge the unfair laws of the day. There were others who used their voices in the streets as protestors and sat down to integrate lunchroom counters. There was even one, the famous Rosa Parks who had worked behind the scenes in the NAACP but she made her mark during the struggle. She simply, yet profoundly sat in front of a public bus refusing to give up her seat to a white man. Every soldier counted. There were some who didn't have a legal degree or money to help finance the movement but their act of serving and resistance was in their passion which was to simply march. The very act in itself became synonymous with the Civil Rights movement. Dr. King's non-violent marching protests were so frequent that one of his naysayers of that time preached a message posing the question, "are we preachers or are we marchers?" Although the march itself was nonviolent, it was often met with great violence. History tells of the story through newspaper articles, photos, and film- a time of gruesome violence that ensued those who desired to peacefully protest the injustices of the south.

One of the most memorable marches of the time was the march in Alabama from the city of Selma to the capital seat of Montgomery. Although the Civil Rights Act of 1964 had ended legal segregation, by 1965, much of the American South had still been successful in suppressing the African American voting population. Alabama was the perfect place for a protest if you wanted to make a statement to America. During this time, Selma held the county seat with a mostly black population and Montgomery was the state's capital. The state was being led out by Governor Corley Wallace who was a known segregationist- opposed to Civil Rights Legislation. Several Civil

83

Rights organizations came together and decided they would march in Alabama.

On March 7, 1965 they gathered in Selma, led out by Civil Rights leader, John Lewis, with approximately 600 marchers. As they marched over the Edmund Pettus Bridge, they were quickly met with opposition. On this first attempt of the march, the participants were met with billy clubs, police on horseback, water hoses, and vicious dogs. This particular day would later be named Bloody Sunday. There were media circulated images of the brutal attacks of the unarmed marchers. Many were injured and hospitalized.

Many times, we recount these historical accounts with poetic language, and they are often romanticized in our minds, but let's be clear, they were real people. During the preparation of this march from Selma, a 26-year-old church deacon and sole provider for his home, Jimmy Lee Jackson who was shot and killed by a state trooper. Reverend James Reeb, a minister and father of four who traveled all the way from Boston only to be beaten to death. Viola Liuzzo a white woman left her husband and five children in Detroit to go all the way to Alabama to march. She felt that she had to make a difference for the world her children were growing up in. As she was transporting a young black marcher back to Selma, the KKK shot into her car. She died from a gunshot wound to the head. After these tragedies and two more attempts, Dr. King along with 8,000 people, mostly black, along with Asians, Latinos, and Whites made to decision to march to Montgomery. Among the religious leaders were Catholic priests, Greek Orthodox bishops and Jewish rabbis. Despite the hardships, dangers, and setbacks, they kept marching.

You may wonder what would make a person put themselves in harm's way? Why after being beat would you then go back to the same bridge to march again? It's called purpose. When you find purpose, it releases a drumbeat at a frequency that at times you're the only one that can hear it. Your sacrifices won't make sense to some and will at times seem crazy to many but keep marching. In Acts 5, the apostles through the power of the Holy Spirit were found healing the sick and preaching about Jesus. The High Priest and the council put them in jail. In the middle of the night they were supernaturally released by an angel of the LORD. The next day they went back to the same area ministering. The council joined together and beat them and commanded them not to speak again in the name of Jesus, but their reply was, "We rather obey God than man." They kept marching for the sake of the message. Dr. King mentioned, in his speech at Selma, a woman by the name of Sister Pollard. Sister Pollard was a 70-year-old woman who participated in the Alabama Bus Boycott. Someone offered her a ride one day and she declined. They asked her, "Aren't you tired?" She answered, "My Feet are tired, but my soul is rested." When you're marching at the cadence of purpose you will sometimes get tired but during those times purpose will give you strength. Hebrews 12:2 says, "for the joy that was set before Jesus, he endured the cross." The pain of the cross was connected to the purpose of redemption for the whole world. They kept marching because they realized that this was bigger than them. Just because you're tired doesn't mean you have to quit. May you find a purpose worth marching for.

Day Twenty-Four
Keep Fighting

One of my favorite movies is The Color Purple. There's a scene in it where the character Sophia, played by Oprah Winfrey, says "You told Harpo to beat me. All my life I had to fight. I had to fight my daddy, my uncles, and my brothers....." Many of us can empathize with these sentiments, for it seems like we've been in some sort of conflict since the earliest stages of our lives. Job 14:1 says "Man that is born of a woman is of few days and full of trouble." This tells us that after we are born, we are soon introduced to some sort of battle. We find ourselves fighting battles that we didn't choose. Although we didn't start it, we may have to consider that we may be called to finish it.

The bible is filled with poetic, romantic, and spiritual literature. But it also includes some of the most action-packed war stories. The entire Old Testament is filled with many series of conflicts between families and nations. Each time the people of Israel found themselves up against the wall, God would raise up a warrior to fight for them. So many of the great men of faith like Abraham, Moses, Joshua and David are considered fighting men. The bible records how they rose to become fighting warriors. God promised the children of Israel the land of Canaan as an inheritance. They possessed the land, but it was done through conquest. Just because something is a promise, it doesn't mean you won't have to fight for it. A promise is more often surrounded by opposition.

Something being surrounded by a fence implies that, what's on the other side of it is very valuable. Many times, we have to fight through high fences of adversity and great walls of depression. There would not be a battle if there were no spoil connected to it. The greater the battle, the greater the victory. In the book of 2 Samuel there was a man by the name of Shammah. We don't know a lot about him, but David honors him as a great man. He lived during a time period when Israel was being constantly terrorized by the Philistines. When the time of the lentil harvest had come, the Philistine army decided to show up. Everyone fled and left the field, except for Shammah. I've learned over the years that at the arrival of a great harvest, the harvest field will become a battlefield. Shammah stood alone against all of the Philistines. He stood until he defeated the entire Philistine troop. What made him stand when everyone else fled? I believe there are divine moments when God gives courage to a willing vessel.

There have been moments in my life that I have stood in bravery with a level of boldness that allowed me to shine above others. Although many gave me great compliments afterward, I had to acknowledge that it wasn't me. I just happened to be the one that made myself available. If you're willing to fight, I believe God will give you the courage. The bible says that Shammah stood in the midst of the field and fought the enemy. This means he didn't run towards the enemy, but he waited for the enemy to come to him. How does one man by the power of the Holy Spirit defeat a whole army? He does it by fighting one man at a time. There are days you will feel like you're fighting all by yourself. Everyone may have retreated or abandoned the assignment of the field you all share. When you start feeling overwhelmed, take a breath and then fight what's in front of you until you have won the whole battle. God is your strength. Zechariah 4:6 says, "Not by might, nor by power, but by my spirit, saith the Lord of hosts."

The New Testament doesn't give us accounts of great battles with the running of great chariots and clanking swords. We are introduced to our Savior who is the Prince of Peace. However, peace is not the absence of conflict, but having peace is remaining in a state of mind in the midst of it. In the new covenant writings, there are still great battles, but the warfare focus is shifted to the spiritual realm.

For we wrestle not against flesh and blood, but against principalities, against powers, against the rulers of the darkness of this world, against spiritual wickedness in high places.

Ephesians 6:12

I will admit there are those who over spiritualize everything; and then there are others who underestimate the negative influences of the spiritual realm. You don't have to believe in spiritual warfare in order to be affected by it. There are things that believers will face that cannot be remedied with natural means.

For the weapons of our warfare are not carnal, but mighty through God to the pulling down of strong holds.

2 Corinthians 2:4

Prayer is our weapon. We don't fight with our hands, but we fight on our knees. Prayer builds a wall of defense and postures us to receive divine war strategies. Prayer is not just speaking to God, but it involves speaking <u>WITH</u> God. In prayer we can speak to mountains of opposition. In prayer we pull down strongholds. Strongholds are thought patterns and demonic systems built up overtime. Consistent prayers will tear those systems down one at a time. It is very easy to get so busy that your prayer life begins to suffer. But we lose battles when we fail to pray.

A military uniform speaks of rank and preparedness. The Apostle Paul tells us that we must be dressed for the battle.

"Wherefore take unto you the whole armour of God, that ye may be able to withstand in the evil day, and having done all, to stand. Stand therefore, having your loins girt about with truth, and having on the breastplate of righteousness;
And your feet shod with the preparation of the gospel of peace;
Above all, taking the shield of faith, wherewith ye shall be able to quench all the fiery darts of the wicked.
And take the helmet of salvation, and the sword of the Spirit, which is the word of God:
Praying always with all prayer and supplication in the Spirit, and watching thereunto with all perseverance and supplication for all saints."

Ephesians 6:13-18

Anytime we mention fighting or war, we automatically start hearing the grunts of testosterone. Men are known for being fighters but there is nothing like a warring woman, especially when it comes to her children. During the time of Israel's famine, there was a woman by the name of Rizpah who had two sons. They were hung for the sins of their father. Rizpah had no control over the situation, but she stayed by the hanging corpses of her sons. Day and night, she stood by them. She fought the birds that would try to pick at their remains and the animals that would try to drag them away. As grief stricken as she was, she was fighting for what was left.

To others it may have been a lost cause, but she was looking at what she had birthed in the Earth. She was fighting for the honor of her sons. She fought for several months until she got the king's attention. King David asked her what she wanted, and she requested that her sons' bodies be buried. The king granted her request and the famine ended. There are times where it will seem that there's not much left of your marriage, ministry, business, vision or academic career; but let the testimony of Rizpah speak to you. Whatever is left is still worth fighting for. Keep fighting until you get the King's attention.

Day Twenty-Five
Keep Getting Up

Those of us who have been in church all of our lives are often called
"pew babies". This nick name refers to all of the years from our
childhood to our adulthood that we've spent within the walls of the
church. We were changed, fed, corrected, and did our homework
either on or under a church pew. I have so many great memories of
these days of being reared by a community of believers. I gave my
life to the LORD and became a believer at a very early age at the
Canaan Land Church in my hometown. I'm going to be honest, I
probably didn't understand what salvation fully was at that point,
but the people who were believers made me want to be one. Their
love for God and the things of God was just contagious. I remember
looking at them as a kid thinking, I want the Holy Ghost and I want
to be just like them, especially Sister Verlie Mae Hunt. Sister Hunt
felt the Holy Ghost every day of the week, even in the grocery store.
The LORD saved me when I was twelve years old. It didn't come
with a certificate or a class, but I knew that something supernatural
had taken place in my heart. I was on fire for God from that moment
and everyone noticed. I followed the examples of the seasoned
saints around me. My church was Pentecostal, so they taught me
how to sing, dance, play instruments, and shout. I also had Sunday
school teachers like Mrs. Goodie Wright who made us learn the 10
Commandments, Beatitudes, The Lord's Prayer, Psalm 100 and
Psalm 23. I still know these scriptures today because of it.

The Classical Pentecostal Holiness Church culture had a very strong
doctrinal teaching on holy living. It still does today. This style of
living was sometimes interpreted through a list of do's and don'ts.
Depending on the pastor and the church, it could include everything
from specific attire requirements to particular acceptable and
unacceptable forms of entertainment. I tried my best to follow the
list and it was pretty easy until I grew up. Remember I was only
twelve. I didn't have a car or puberty. I lived in my mother's home,
so church was my only option. As I began to mature, I quickly
realized that although my soul was saved, salvation did not negate
the fact that I still had to undergo the same stages of life as everyone
else.

When I found out I was human, I was shocked, disappointed and grieved. Through my church and natural family, I was taught extensively how to live "right." I didn't know that in my humanity I was going to have an inevitable moment where I realized that I was human after all. I was grieved because after considering all of what God had done for me, I had let Him down. As a young believer I became confused. In our worship services people would get up and testify about how they were Saved, Sanctified and Filled with the Holy Ghost. They would stand and report how God had used them to do great things. Even the songs would make reference to how they had been having Jesus on their mind all day. No one would get up and testify about how they had failed, made mistakes, and missed the mark. This made me believe that maybe I didn't get the real Holy Ghost. Maybe I had a cheap counterfeit or maybe I had conjured up an emotional moment in my head. I felt this way because I was experiencing failures that no other believer was experiencing, so I thought. So, for the next several years I could never be confident in my salvation. I would respond to every altar call, no matter the denomination, just in case.

My relationship with God was based upon performance. I thought God's love for me was totally based upon how well I was keeping the rules at the time. I didn't understand the concept of His unconditional love. To be honest, I still don't fully understand it but every chance I get, I open myself to receive it. Maybe because I didn't grow up with a father, I didn't understand a father's love. In Luke 15, Jesus tells a story about a father who had two sons. The younger son asked for his inheritance and the father gave it to him. He left his father's house, went to another country, and wasted all of his money. He failed. He became so hungry and desperate that he prepared himself to eat with the pigs until he came to himself. What brought him back to himself was the memory of his father's house. He returned and before he made it all the way back home, the father prepared a change of garments and a feast for him. The father embraced him and declared that his son had returned home. For many years I've known this story as the prodigal son. The word prodigal means reckless. However, when I read the scripture the father never called him prodigal, he called him son. This story is really not about the son, but it's about how the father sees us even when we fall. When the youngest was at home, he was his father's son. When he went into a far country and partied, he was his father's son. When he got down to eat the pig slop, he was still his father's son. When he returned, the narrative didn't change, he called him son. You may have grown up in church and sung the songs of praise. Maybe you fell from grace and decided just to stay away. May the memories of your father's house bring you back to him.

The history of the Israelites tells us over and over that what you don't kill can come back and attack you later. As I accepted my call to ministry, I was convinced that I had outgrown any potential shortcomings of my past. There is no greater let down than to find yourself repeating things you felt that you were free of and delivered from. I felt like a total hypocrite not because people found out, but because God and I knew it. I've always loved God. From my perspective, He had honored me to be a preacher, therefore, at least I could live for Him. I cried and pleaded with God to take away any weakness out of my life.

Three different times I begged the Lord to take it away. Each time he said, "My grace is all you need. My power works best in weakness." So now I am glad to boast about my weaknesses, so that the power of Christ can work through me.

2 Corinthians 12: 8-10

Apostle Paul said he had a thorn that he asked God to remove three times. I had Paul beat, I asked at least a hundred times. Scholars have been hypothesizing for years concerning the identity of Paul's thorn in his flesh. I, on the other hand, am glad it was never named because we would have placed his thorn in an isolated category. God's response to his request, is the same as ours, His grace is enough. His grace is there to keep us from falling and to recover us when we do.

God is not disappointed. Bishop Ralph Donnie Graves said, "God can be displeased but never disappointed because He's omniscient." When I heard this statement, it was liberating. There were times in my life when I shocked myself by some of the reckless decisions that I had made. Then I was reminded, God knows me. This means before He called me, He already took into account my flaws, strengths, weaknesses, and proclivities. What is mind boggling to me is that an immutable God, that contains a priceless treasure, in which He purchased with His great sacrifice, has entrusted it to mere feeble and weak men.

But we have this treasure in earthen vessels, that the excellency of the power may be of God, and not of us.

2 Corinthians 4:7

Jesus told Peter that the enemy wanted to destroy him but that He had already prayed that his faith would not fail him (Luke 22:31-32). Jesus didn't pray that Peter would not fail because He already knew that he was going to fall. He prayed that Peter's faith would survive it. I believe nothing grieves the Holy Spirit more than our lack of faith to receive His forgiveness. Christ died and rose again for us to be forgiven. But we allow condemnation to block us from receiving it.

I wanted to walk away from the ministry- but not because of the assignment. I love the assignment of preaching and teaching, but the weight of the responsibility had become too much. I knew I had a responsibility to live this life in front of the people and I felt like a failure, even if they didn't know. I understood my responsibility was to always be ready to preach, teach, pray, be a visionary, eat right, exercise, visit the sick, bury the dead, encourage, correct, love, and NEVER sin. WHO CAN DO THIS? I decided if I couldn't do this right, I didn't want to do it at all. As I looked around me, I realize there were many people who could trust me with their secrets, but I wondered who could I trust with mine? This posture of non-confessing had me serving and consistently falling. This is how believers end up deeper in sin because sin festers in darkness. This means we go deeper into sin when we feel there's no one we can confide in. I came up with different strategies to escape this responsibility because failure was too much for me to bear. Every time I tried to execute an exit plan, I would see my family and my church who had always stood by me and believed in my ministry. At random moments I would receive an email or social media message telling me that my ministry changed their lives. Some even confided in telling me that my ministry kept them from committing suicide. It blew my mind because some of the messages they were referring to had actually been preached at some of my lowest moments.

Where can I go from Your Spirit?
Or where can I flee from Your presence?
If I ascend into heaven, You are there;
If I make my bed in hell, behold, You are there.
If I take the wings of the morning,
And dwell in the uttermost parts of the sea,
Even there Your hand shall lead me,
And Your right hand shall hold me.

Psalm 139

I believe in generational curses. The more I talk to my father, the more I learn about me. My temptation with sexual lusts and sudden urges for alcohol consumption was something that I inherited. This goes back many generations in my family. I don't believe we should use generational curses as an excuse for bondage. But we should use them as a personal case studies on our family's strongholds. Identifying these patterns gives us leverage in prayer. This is why today I teach our parishioners against social drinking. I believe it would prove ineffective to try to bring forth freedom from something that we are inebriated with.

This entry is not intended to be a deliverance manual or to glorify sin, but it is intended to let someone know that your failure is not final. I wanted to give the testimony that I didn't hear growing up. I wanted to stand and say, "Praise the Lord everybody, I fell but I got back up!" Today I stand and preach with confidence knowing that I'm not a hypocrite. I live the life I preach about. I live all of it, the ups and the downs. We have created a church culture that teaches people how to stand but has failed to teach the same people how to recover. If I show people my accomplishments without acknowledging my failures, then I'll be receiving glory that only belongs to God. Today I'm standing not because I've never failed, but because I've failed enough to learn how to stand. People may know your failure, but God knows your repentance. God has not changed his mind about you. Keep Getting Up!

The steps of a good man are ordered by the Lord: and he delighteth in his way.
Though he fall, he shall not be utterly cast down: for the Lord upholdeth him with his hand.

Psalm 37:23-24

For a just man falleth seven times, and riseth up again: but the wicked shall fall into mischief.

Proverbs 24:16

Day Twenty-Six
No Reference Point

I've often wondered many times before how did we ever travel without GPS? I've become so dependent on navigational apps that I've even used them in my local area to ensure I'm using the fastest route home. Before these Global Positioning Systems came into existence, we used maps and human directions. In a rural area, it wasn't uncommon to hear someone give directions by mentioning landmarks such as the big tree or the white house on the corner with black shutters. Modern technology has spoiled us with not only up-to-date directions, but it also gives us the exact time we will arrive. Many of us love being in control. We all know that person or we are that person whether in the driver's seat, passenger seat, or the back seat-they need to be in charge. They will try to control everything from the direction of the vehicle, to the music that's being played. Walking with God becomes a great challenge for people of control because God often sends us in the direction of our destiny without a lot of details. God told Abraham to leave his family and country and go to a land where He will show him. The only challenge with this command is that he was told to go without being told where. When you have a command from God without a lot of information just move in the direction of His voice.

For we walk by faith, not by sight.

2 Corinthians 5:7

Sometimes thinking we know what God wants without hearing Him can cause us to error. There's nothing wrong with the instructions God gave you yesterday. Just make sure that what He is still saying concerns your life today. Jesus told the disciples in Matthew 6 to pray, "Give us THIS day our daily bread." When we fail to keep our ears to the lips of God, we risk being loyal to a diet of stale bread. Jehovah told Israel to walk around the walls of Jericho every day, one time, for 6 days in silence. I could imagine by day seven most of them felt they already knew how this exercise and routine would go down. However, the seventh day was different. They were commanded to walk around the wall seven times and end it with a shout. When they shouted, the walls of Jericho came down. Maybe some of us still have walls up in our lives because we went home too early. Perhaps, we ended our walk too soon.

Remember the former things of old: [a]for I am God, and there is none else; I am God, and there is none like me; [10] declaring the end from the beginning, and from ancient times things that are not yet done; saying, My counsel shall stand, and I will do all my pleasure;
Isaiah 46:9-10 American Standard Version (ASV)

"Remember not the former things, nor consider the things of old. Behold, I am doing a new thing; now it springs forth, do you not perceive it? I will make a way in the wilderness and rivers in the desert.
Isaiah 43:18-19 English Standard Version (ESV)

Reading the book of Isaiah can leave you feeling confused without proper context. In one verse, we are commanded to remember and in the other verse we are commanded to forget. What I believe is being communicated to us is that we should remember those things that will increase our faith necessary for the next season; but forget those things that would hinder us from going forward. Isaiah 43:19 tells us that God is going to do a new thing, but it also implies that it may be possible to miss it.

How can someone miss a God-thing? People miss God-moments when they master His methods instead of watching for His moves. The children of Israel were in Egypt for 400 years. When they finally made it out, they looked back at Egypt and remembered the food but failed to remember the bondage. We do this with old relationships, churches, jobs, and seasons. We prayed for GOD to move us out of toxic environments but when He does it, we start complaining. We quickly start comparing the challenging things in the new place to the good things of old.

Our church is coming up on 15 years old. It's been a quick and long journey, if that makes sense. We have moved seven times over the span of our short history. Some of those moves were chosen and one of them were forced. There's something I have noticed about our church over the years. Every time we moved, no matter the location or the esthetics of the property, there were always those who claimed that the worship experience was better in the last place. It didn't matter if the roof was leaking or the HVAC was broken. According to the testimonies of the people, God was stronger in the old place in comparison to the new. We all have a tendency to glamorize the past; but we must learn how to praise God for it while looking forward. When driving, if your focus is behind you, you will either miss your turn or have a wreck.

After being in the wilderness for 40 years, I'm pretty sure the children of Israel had covered most of the area, but Canaan remained unknown to them. It was time to crossover into the promised land, but Moses was dead, and Joshua was the new leader. Under Moses' administration, they crossed the Red Sea with him holding up his rod. But the crossing of the Jordan was different. God told Joshua to get the priests and the ark of God and have them to step into the river Jordan. The people were to FOLLOW after the ark of GOD, not the other way around. Why would they need to follow the ark of GOD? The ark was a symbol of God's presence. From this we can learn that when we are in a new place in our life, we can't attempt to approach it without His presence. In Joshua 3:3-4 the LORD tells Joshua to go after the ark of God for, "you have never passed this way before." A new place can be a scary place but having no reference point is not always a bad thing. If you look around and you see no one in your family or community doing what you feel you are called to do, don't abandon it just to fit in.You could be a trailblazer. You may not have a reference point but keep going. You very well may become someone else's.

Chapter Twenty-Seven
Keep Dreaming

A dream is a cherished desire, ambition, or idea. Most of us had them in our younger years- until we grew up. Growing up has a tendency to rob us of some of our most innocent and extreme imaginations. As children, we all had that dream factor that made us believe that anything was possible. As a child, I remember sitting on the back of my grandfather's pick-up truck with my cousins. As we would pass by many homes and vehicles, we would point out the ones we claimed as ours. We were so serious in staking our claims that we would sometimes end up in a quarrel, saying, "I saw it first!" This exclamatory statement would usually be the first line of defense. We believed it was just that easy.

I do not believe we lose that dream factor, as we get older. I just think it breaks down. Anything will break down and become simplified over time when it's not maintained properly. I believe that our dream factors come from God. It's the imaginative aspect of our being that always sees the potential of things being better and greater. I purchased a landscape waterfall fountain for my yard some years ago. One of the guys from the church assembled it for me and filled it up with the water. When we plugged it up, we stood in anticipation for the water to start flowing. Moments later we realized that something wasn't right. The fountain was not working-so we thought. I prepared to repackage it in the box and return it to the store. But, all of sudden I looked down and realized that the water pump wasn't even in the water. The water pump needed to be placed in the water if the fountain was going to work properly. Our dream factors work in the same way. Dream factors can only function in atmospheres that are conducive.

Environment is everything. Just like trees, and certain animals, your dreams can only thrive in particular atmospheres. You are either surrounded by dream killers or dream pushers. Dream killers are people who think you are dreaming too big. They believe that you, as the dreamer, are not being realistic. Dream pushers are those who will encourage you to move in the progressive direction of your dreams. They may not understand your dream, but they will still support your attempts in trying to make your dream a reality.

I don't believe every dream comes from GOD. Just because it is something you desire, it does not mean it is something God desires. I do believe when an aspiration has stayed with you throughout the changes of many seasons, there's a good chance that it is inspired by God. These are what I call prophetic dreams. The only challenge with prophetic dreams is that the dreamer sometimes lacks prophetic perception and fails to understand the importance of timing. Perception deals with the understanding of the dream. Many prophetic dreams deal with symbolic meanings. Some of the people in the dream may simply be a representative of someone or something else. When Joseph dreamed about the sun, moon, and stars, these were actually symbols representing his family. Prophetic timing is sometimes the most complicated and complex to comprehend. Have you ever had a dream and it seemed so real that you actually thought it was going to happen? The dream seemed so real; you could sense it had the possibility to happen immediately or in the very near future. Prophetic dreams can sometimes cause someone to feel that what they've been dreaming is for immediate manifestation. This misunderstanding of prophetic timing can cause frustration and discouragement. In his dream, Joseph saw himself elevated in a high place, but the dream did not reveal the pit, the slavery, and the prison experiences he had to endure first. This tells us God always does what He says He's going to do, but it doesn't always look like what we think it should be. We often times are not privy to the specific details and timing. Joseph had his dream at the age of 17. However, his dream was fulfilled at the age of 40. Once Joseph left his father's land, he ended up in Egypt. Notice the bible never mentions him dreaming a new dream while in Egypt. The circumstances around him changed, but the same dream remained. Don't ever stop dreaming. Mature, advance, increase, expand; but never remove the part of you that has the ability to dream. The fulfillment of Joseph's dream ended up saving other people's lives. Dream big enough so that others can live the dream along with you. Keep Dreaming.

"Now to him who is able to do immeasurably more than all we ask or imagine, according to his power that is at work within us."
Ephesians 3:20

Chapter Twenty-Eight
Keep Singing

Most of our greatest memories have a soundtrack that is connected to it. There's a song for every occasion. We all have a playlist of songs that we refer to as "our jam". When you hear that particular song, your mind goes back to a particular time and space. Music truly is therapy and singing in particular is cathartic. Many of us can perform whole concerts in the shower. Others of us have been known to blast our voices on the highway, just as loud as the speakers in our car. We all sing. We may not all sing professionally or as skillfully as others, but we all do it. Scientific studies prove that endorphins, also known as feel-good chemicals are released in our brains when we sing. This means there's more to singing than having fun. Here are some benefits:
1. It releases stress.
2. It helps your memory.
3. Makes your heart stronger.
4. Gives you energy.

If we receive all of this when we sing, it can be concluded that we can lose some of these benefits when we stop.

When a person loses their song, it signifies that something bad has taken place. Problems and disappointments can come to rob us of our melody. We can go from singing loud one day to living on mute the next day. There was a time in Israeli history when Jerusalem lost its song. The people of Israel were seized by the Babylonians. Soon after, a great number of Jews were exiled to Babylon. The place of Babylon was a strange place with a different religious culture. To make matters worse, Babylon was a long distance from Jerusalem, their home and the epicenter of their worship. One psalmist in Psalm 137 reminisces of that time period:

By the rivers of Babylon, there we sat down, yea, we wept, when we remembered Zion.
We hanged our harps upon the willows in the midst thereof.

For there they that carried us away captive required of us a song; and they that wasted us required of us mirth, saying, Singus one of the songs of Zion.
How shall we sing the Lord's song in a strange land?

I can only imagine what it felt like to be displaced and separated from home and then be requested to sing. They weren't just asked to sing, but they were required to sing a Zion song. No doubt the Babylonians enjoyed the sound of the Jews singing. To the Babylonians, their singing was entertainment, but for the Jews it was worship. They responded to the request with a question, "How can we sing the Lord's song in a strange land?" What they were really asking was, how can we worship God this far from the temple? How can we sing in this type of situation? There are moments in our lives where singing would be considered inappropriate for the circumstance. Maybe you feel like the people of Israel who were exiled. After pondering your situation and your surroundings you may resolve that you have nothing to sing about. Where you are may be far from your Jerusalem. Perhaps, the song will bring Jerusalem to you instead.

One proponent of slavery attempted to prove that the African slaves were happy in bondage because the slaves were always seen singing while working in the field. The observer who made this statement made singing synonymous with being happy. Although singing can be a sign of happiness, it is not limited to those kinds of moments. For the slaves, singing was a means of survival. Singing helped them endure the back-breaking days of working from sun-up to sun-down. Singing gave them strength and hope. History also taught us that singing was the secret language of the Underground Railroad. What the slave master thought was just cultural moaning and religious rhetoric was actually a secret communication about escaping to the north in freedom. In the same manner, there's a spiritual language in singing. Apostle Paul said that he would sing with the spirit and sing with the understanding also (1 Corinthians 14:15). This denotes another mode of spiritual singing you can experience in an unlearned language that even you yourself don't understand. Remember you don't have to understand something in order for it to work for you.

102

How singing takes place through the anatomy of our bodies is a miracle in and of itself. On the surface you may think singing simply comes through the manipulation of the larynx. This couldn't be further from the truth. In order to sing, it takes the stomach muscles, the rib cage, the lungs, the oral cavity, and even your back muscles. Taking this into consideration, it takes the coordination of all these compartments to fall into perfect sequence. We then must conclude that the ability to sing on any level is a divine miracle. When we lift our voices to sing, we are actually activating the miraculous power of God within us.

Speaking to yourselves in psalms and hymns and spiritual songs, singing and making melody in your heart to the Lord.

Ephesians 5:19

 Have you ever walked around singing a tune and didn't even know you were singing? That's because music, the lyrics, the tune, or melody gets into your soul. Your soul is comprised of your mind, will, and emotions. There are moments when a song is trapped into the depths of your being and it needs to be released. If secular or fun-filled singing renders us stress relieving benefits, how much more will the song of the Lord release unto us? Your song may be a song that hasn't been penned or recorded. It can simply be lyrics coined from your heart to the heart of God. You may not be where you want to be in life but create a playlist for the journey and keep singing.

I will sing unto the LORD as long as I live: I will sing praise to my God while I have my being.

Psalm 104:33

Day Twenty-Nine
Keep Waiting

Modern technology has afforded this generation with many comforts. Things that used to take a long time to produce are now able to take place within minutes, sometimes even seconds. As a result, this fast-paced culture has become obsessed with presentation-void of an understanding of process. Things of great quality don't just appear, but they are manufactured over time. When you go to a restaurant and order a steak, there's an understanding that it will not come out of the kitchen as quickly as other items on the menu. It takes longer to cook. Therefore, it requires a longer period of waiting.

No one desires to wait.
This is obvious if you were to observe the grocery store check-out lines. You will find disgruntled customers waiting in long lines. Your ability to wait exposes your level of maturity. Everything in our carnal nature desires instant gratification, but spiritual maturation understands the concept of seasons and timing. Out of Jesus' words, it is possible we have overlooked His response to His mother at the wedding at Cana. When she asked Jesus to do something about the wine shortage, He responded, "My time is not yet." Jesus was teaching us that the presence of ability is not always indicative of an immediate action. It all has to do with timing. For example, a young woman experiencing a menstrual cycle speaks of her ability to give birth, but it doesn't mean it's her time. The more we understand God's timing, the more we are willing to wait. Mature believers in waiting understand that in God something that is delayed doesn't mean it's denied.

The problem some people have with waiting, is that time is our most precious commodity. Once a day is gone, no one can go back and reclaim it. No one wants to be caught waiting for something that's never going to happen. Let's be clear, there is no time wasted when you're waiting on God. Waiting on God creates a greater ability to endure. Your endurance muscle is strengthened when waiting. Waiting gives you space to ensure that you are receiving clear directions from God. Waiting also gives us a greater appreciation for things. When things quickly happen for us, we have a tendency to devalue and dishonor it. The prophet Isaiah says that we are in some way strengthened in our process of waiting.

"Yet those who wait for the LORD will gain new strength; They will mount up with wings like eagles, They will run and not get tired, They will walk and not become weary."

Isaiah 40:31

It is important to remember that God is sovereign and absolute in His authority. The truth of the matter is, there will be times that regardless of what you say or do; you will not be able to force God into doing anything quicker than He desires. Without any other options, you are forced to wait. During these moments, the focus is not on the fact that you're waiting, the focus should be centered more on HOW you choose to wait. David said in Isaiah 40:1, "I waited patiently for the LORD; and He inclined unto me and heard my cry." In this scripture, waiting is the action, but David's attitude was an attitude that demonstrated patience. How have YOU been waiting? What has your attitude been during the waiting periods of your life? Some people have been guilty of complaining and fussing throughout their entire waiting period. This type of attitude communicates that you have not yet reached a maturity level that is able to handle what you have asked for. A complaining and impatient attitude will cause our process of waiting to be elongated.

As a believer waiting on God, we should posture ourselves in praise to God. The decision to wait is a reflection of how you perceive God's character. Your decision to wait communicates that you believe that God is trustworthy. Who would continuously wait on someone whose track record has been proven unreliable? It would seem foolish to do this. When we wait on God with patience and joy, it bears witness, even to the unbeliever that, our God is dependable. Our ability to wait and trust God shows how much we value Him. When there are other options and alternatives that appear to be easier, our decision to trust in God is tested and challenged. The Bible advises us to, "Trust in the Lord with all thine heart; and lean not unto thine own understanding" (Proverbs 3:5).

God is an eternal being who is not affected by time. As a matter of fact, time was not made for God. Time was made for man. Anything God desires to do, in all actuality has already been completed in Him and in eternity. Isaiah 46:10 says, "Declaring the end from the beginning, and from ancient times the things that are not yet done, saying, My counsel shall stand, and I will do all my pleasure." Considering this truth, our waiting on God is really more about us than it has to do with Him. Anyone who has ever been used mightily by God has gone through a season of waiting. Esther underwent a whole year of preparation before being chosen by the king. Joseph had a dream when he was 17 years old concerning his elevation to the palace. He didn't arrive to the palace until he was 40 years old. Moses was 40 years old when he left Egypt; and was 80 years old when God spoke to him to return for His purpose. Waiting should not be considered as an idle pastime. Waiting should be considered as a time of preparation for what lies ahead. Waiting serves as preparation for a greater moment. If you're waiting on God, do not consider this waiting as a punishment or indictment. Instead, know that you are standing in His preparation.

Although I was never that of a good of a student, in my opinion, I always had aspirations to go to college. My mentor, Pastor Burnell Baize always encouraged me to apply to Liberty University, so, in 1997 I did. Unfortunately, after applying and calling the admissions office, and not receiving an acceptance letter, I learned that I was not accepted. To say the least, I was very disappointed. Nevertheless, I chose to move on and enter the workforce and volunteer in ministry. After six years of working in retail, I decided to apply to Liberty University again. After many nerve wrecking weeks, I received the news that I had finally been accepted. In the fall of 2003, I started my freshman year at the world's largest Christian university, Liberty University. I was so excited. I was given a photo ID with a student identification number. Often, I would be required to provide my student ID number in the cafeteria, library, and other places across campus. When I would provide my number, which was 925, the official would always ask for the rest of the numbers, implying that my ID number was invalid. To prove that I was a student, I would always have to pull out my ID card to assure them that my student number really was 925. I finally understood the official's suspicion regarding my ID number. Everyone else had five numbers or more. I only had three. In 2005 as a college student, I started my church in the living room of my duplex apartment. My first secretary in our small church was Flora Lazo who worked in the admissions office at the university. One day I asked her why my ID number was so small compared to the other students. She did some research and came back to me with her astonishing find. According to the records, I was accepted to attend the university in 1997. The notes in my student file mistakenly documented that I had not responded and the number 925 was issued to my account in 1997 when I originally applied. WOW! All this time I thought I was rejected. I had been accepted after all. When I tell this story, many people think this would make me angry, but my feelings are quite the opposite. I praise GOD with everything in me. I realized that if I would have come to the university in 1997, I would've missed my time of preparation that was afforded to me in the retail store and volunteering in ministry. Even more, I would've missed the whole generation of people who became the founding charter members of our church and movement. I'm glad it didn't happen when I wanted it. I'm glad I waited. Keep Waiting!

Day Thirty
Keep Going

This devotional book was actually inspired by a Sunday Morning service at our church. In an attempt to transition the worship service to the offering, I approached the podium. At that moment an unscripted message came forth. I'm now convinced it was the LORD. I had no idea that a one-minute clip would go viral. Very soon we were bombarded with countless emails and social media messages concerning the message in that video. May you read these simple lines, and may it be strength to your soul.

"I know what it is to cry until you have no tears left."

"But after you finish crying get up and keep going."

"If you're battling depression, let depression know you're not going to keep me immobile."

"I'm going to Keep Going!"

"You who have been under pressure, turn your pressure into praise and Keep Going."

"For you who have made mistakes in your life and the enemy is holding guilt over your head, you will outlive what the Devil said about you…. Keep Going!"